# Building Trust

# Building Trust

## Doing Research to Understand Ethnic Communities

Fumiko Hosokawa

LEXINGTON BOOKS

*A division of*

ROWMAN & LITTLEFIELD PUBLISHERS, INC.
*Lanham • Boulder • New York • Toronto • Plymouth, UK*

Published by Lexington Books
A division of Rowman & Littlefield Publishers, Inc.
A wholly owned subsidiary of The Rowman & Littlefield Publishing Group, Inc.
4501 Forbes Boulevard, Suite 200, Lanham, Maryland 20706
http://www.lexingtonbooks.com

Estover Road, Plymouth PL6 7PY, United Kingdom

British Library Cataloguing in Publication Information Available

**Library of Congress Cataloging-in-Publication Data**

Hosokawa, Fumiko.
  Building trust : doing research to understand ethnic communities / Fumiko Hosokawa.
      p. cm.
  Includes bibliographical references and index.
  ISBN 978-0-7391-4349-0 (cloth : alk. paper) — ISBN 978-0-7391-4350-6 (pbk. : alk. paper) — ISBN 978-0-7391-4351-3 (electronic)
  1. Minorities—United States—Social conditions. 2. Immigrants—United States—Social conditions. 3. United States—Social conditions. I. Title.
  E184.A1H663 2010
  305.800973—dc22           2009035999

⊚ ™ The paper used in this publication meets the minimum requirements of American National Standard for Information Sciences—Permanence of Paper for Printed Library Materials, ANSI/NISO Z39.48-1992.

Printed in the United States of America

# Contents

# Preface

It took ten years to write this book, but that may not be such a long time in the evolution of ideas. Beginning with a grant project to study ethnic groups in their own communities, the project produced a manual on how to train people to do fieldwork in these communities. This manual was disseminated to agencies in the surrounding communities of California State University–Dominguez Hills, as well as to various individuals on this campus. One of these individuals was Professor Don Hata, who requested a copy of the manual and used it in his history courses. Don Hata's comment to me was the inspiration for my writing this book—he said the manual should be published because he found it valuable as a teaching tool.

Don Hata has long been retired but his words stayed with me over the years. I did intend to turn the manual into a book, but I did not know when I would do so. Soon after I finished the grant project, I decided to become a Marriage and Family Therapist. This required two and a half years of education leading to a second Master's degree and a few years of internship before I received my license to do counseling. The counseling career became an adjunct to my full-time teaching at Cal State–Dominguez Hills.

Eventually, I found my way back to the book and gradually developed it until it built its own momentum. The last three chapters didn't take anywhere near the time it took to do the first seven chapters. The years spent doing other things only broadened the experience and knowledge that could be applied to the book. This was necessary to create a final product that went way beyond the original manual and that could be useful in a wider context.

I wish to thank my former colleague, Emeritus Professor Don Hata, for giving me the encouragement to follow through with this book. Don represents the best in university teaching, and he is a champion of minority rights. Other acknowledgments go to Paul Chikahisa, Sandy Orellana, and Ken Kuykendall. Mr. Chikahisa's assistance was necessary in developing the basic guidelines in doing fieldwork in chapter 2. He was a Field Instructor at the Asian American Community Mental Health Training Center in Los Angeles during the 1970s and 1980s. Dr. Sandy Orellana's assistance in developing the step-by-step procedures for doing fieldwork advising in chapter 2 is greatly appreciated. She is a retired professor of anthropology at Cal State–Dominguez Hills, who is still teaching part time. Dr. Ken Kuykendall was a professor of anthropology also at Cal State–Dominguez Hills, who has been retired for some time. I am indebted to him for helping develop the section on the nature of communities in chapter 5: Ethnic Groups and Communities. Lastly, I would like to thank my colleague in the sociology department, Professor Matt Mutchler, for reading and critiquing a draft of this book. Professor Mutchler's encouragement and positive comments were refreshing to hear, especially his comment to find a publisher that will give the book wide dissemination so that many students can read it.

No one has had more influence in my writing than my late mother, Teruko Hosokawa. Not only was she a teacher, artist, motivator, and guide, she was the "wind beneath my wings." I dedicate this book to her knowing that her spirit will share my joy in its completion. I know she would appreciate the basic theme of this book, which is to build relationships and community ties in the pursuit of higher education.

**Fumiko Hosokawa**

# Chapter 1

# Introduction

Ethnic groups are fascinating to study because they help us become familiar with cultural beliefs, styles of communication, and social behaviors that are different from our own. They broaden our perspective of the world and allow us to experience many new things that go beyond the confines of our own culture. We can learn about ethnic groups in such diverse ways as visiting a foreign country, interacting with individual members of an ethnic group in our communities, or at work, or by just reading about them through a sociology or anthropology course. We do have many textbooks written on ethnic groups in our society from a sociological, historical, anthropological, or political point of view that help us get various perspectives on these groups. However, when one studies ethnic groups directly by going out into their communities, the information one acquires about them is surprisingly different and extremely valuable.

As an instructor of sociology race and ethnic relations courses, the author had plenty of textbook knowledge about how ethnic communities operated and how much diversity there was through cultural differences. What she didn't have was an insider's knowledge of what people thought about others who were different from their own ethnic group and how they would behave toward them based on these thoughts. The author was interested in this information because, as a sociologist, she valued fieldwork observations and found that getting firsthand information from people was more useful than simply reading a general textbook on race relations. Fieldwork can be defined as the activity of observing people in their natural environment so that one can gain intimate insights into their behavior and be able to report these insights social scientifically in ways that are not harmful to the people (Junker 1960, iii). However, one of the problems in doing fieldwork with ethnic populations

1

is being able to collect accurate data about the groups. The author knew that cultural differences between the researcher and the subjects would be a strong factor affecting data collection. Other factors exist, too, but this particular one seemed to be very important because it affects one's rapport with a group and the interview style that evolves from interactions. Her concern was how one could collect data from ethnic group members that were representative of their beliefs, lifestyles, culture, and behaviors.

The author applied for a grant while teaching at California State University–Dominguez Hills in Carson, California, in 1979, so that she could explore this idea and come up with some information that would be useful to individuals who do fieldwork in ethnic communities. The information could be useful to others, too, such as business leaders, government officials, and anyone who would have reason to interact with members in ethnic communities. The grant proposal did result in funding, and this lead to the author's Pilot Ethnic Research Training Project. The data that were collected from this grant project, which deals with responses from several different ethnic groups about researchers, is the basis for this book. Despite this material being collected at an earlier time period, it is still relevant today. The cultural beliefs and values that were identified would be relevant today because traditional cultures don't change that much when people first immigrate to a new country, especially when these values are upheld by the older generation. Also, these immigrants try to preserve beliefs and rituals that can easily get threatened by extinction from the larger culture.

When we are looking at American ethnic groups, their beliefs and behaviors are sometimes a response to how they are treated by the dominant group, and their attitudes reflect strains in inter-group relations that remain long after assimilation has taken place. Therefore, tapping into these responses would continue to be relevant long after the first generation of immigrants has settled here, especially in knowing how to improve ethnic relations.

Understanding minority groups and their culture is important even if one were not doing research on these groups. Visitors to foreign countries are aware of ethnic values and norms when they unintentionally violate them. They may not be aware of how they have offended their hosts, but they can see the consequences. Sometimes the consequences are as severe as imprisonment, as in the case of bringing drugs into a country; or, the consequences can result in angry glares or hostile behavior. Knowing a group's culture will help people avoid situations that could lead to negative interaction.

On American soil there is a tendency to assume that ethnic groups will rapidly assimilate and be quite westernized after a number of years. The tendency to standardize people into Americans makes it easy to overlook cultural and historical differences about them. When these differences are overlooked during the research process, it is easy to get inadequate or false information about people. It can also lead to incomplete information about a group that will affect the ability to deliver much needed community services.

This book was written to identify the problems in doing fieldwork in ethnic communities with both immigrant and Americanized ethnic groups in the United States. Knowing that researchers have gone out to ethnic neighborhoods for years to gather information, the author was not interested in how they do fieldwork, but in knowing how accurate their data would be if there were cultural and racial differences between researcher and subject. Using the approach of interviewing subjects about researchers in their community makes this book unique. The intent of the book is not to criticize the fieldwork of others or the tools that researchers use, but to examine the process of fieldwork in ethnic communities as a complicated venture that may require much collaboration between researcher and subject before it can be successful.

The author also had another reason for writing this book. She is especially interested in any study that can contribute to a greater understanding of prejudice and discrimination between ethnic groups, as well as finding ways to reduce ethnic conflict. It was LaPiere's landmark study that brings this area to mind. If contact can reduce prejudice because face-to-face interaction makes people more humanistic and less discriminatory (LaPiere 1934), then an ethnographic fieldwork approach to working with ethnic people would seem to clarify misconceptions about them. It might even make the ethnic communities more tolerant of strangers who want to study them, get to know them for various reasons, or interact with them on an ongoing basis.

The material for this book was initially developed as part of a grant project entitled, The Pilot Ethnic Research Training Project, which was funded by the Office of Education in 1979. The project consisted of training faculty members to do fieldwork in the African American, Southeast Asian, Japanese American, Mexican American, and Samoan communities, and creating a directory of ethnic community agencies representative of these five groups. A fieldwork manual was also a project goal, and this manual was intended to not only clarify the roles of advisor and supervisor to the student doing fieldwork in ethnic communities, but to develop ways to implement curriculum materials and research ideas in the community.

However, after the fieldwork manual was completed and disseminated, the author found that there was so much information lacking about the ethnic people themselves, as well as resources on how to understand ethnic communities from a research point of view, that she decided to follow up, years later, with this book. Unlike the earlier manual, this book focuses on the cultural meanings and expectations of ethnic community members—a group that is usually minimized in fieldwork texts. Because the author considered the views of these individuals to be critical in the successful implementation of research ideas, she spent a good deal of time getting information from these individuals with the assistance of consultants who conducted interviews with community members. (See the appendix for a list of interview questions used in collecting data.) This data is presented and analyzed in the second half of the text to help the reader learn about fieldwork as a negotiable process.

The particular approach the author is using is a humanistic one because it attempts to bring the world of the ethnic community into view and to let the people in these communities be their own voice. The perceptions and opinions of these community members may not only provide insights and new information to the reader, but also an understanding of the sentiment of ethnic individuals when they are encountering researchers in their midst. What is presented, then, is a study of the protocols of fieldwork in ethnic communities with both empirical and theoretical concerns being examined. This implies that fieldwork is not simply a general activity that results in data collection but a serious endeavor that can be tedious or routine at times, but also enlightening and adventurous.

The interview data used in this book would be difficult to generalize to other populations in the United States. This is because the sample size was very small and nonrandom and included both responses from agency directors and ethnic community members. These individuals can be broken down into the following ethnicities: twenty African Americans, five Lao community members, ten Vietnamese Chinese, ten Vietnamese, twenty-two Japanese Americans, twenty-two Mexican Americans, and twenty Samoans. All of these individuals were from neighborhoods in Southern California, especially in Los Angeles County, and the communities around California State University–Dominguez Hills, which is in Carson.

The information these respondents gave became a wonderful supplement to academic knowledge. It made the author realize that classroom theory is not enough to get the student through fieldwork assignments or to really understand ethnic communities. Students and other individuals need some guidance on how to approach people who are different from them culturally and racially, because these individuals could easily have different views from their own about research problems and data interpretation. It is the author's hope that information from this book will be sufficient to give even the novice student or practitioner the necessary tools for understanding ethnic individuals. It would also be beneficial to help others avoid the embarrassments and futile efforts that going blindly into ethnic communities can produce.

This book is broken down into a number of sections. Part I focuses on basic guidelines for doing fieldwork followed by fieldwork supervision and the ethics of doing fieldwork in ethnic communities. It is concerned with how students or staff can be guided by supervisors or other professionals in the activity of interacting with clients or respondents, learning how to relate to them one-on-one, and doing interviews to gather data. The author provides a definition of supervision and mentions the types of individuals who would be in this role. This section is presented to clarify the relationship between supervisor and supervisee.

Following this section, supervisory techniques and practices are mentioned. They include the role of community agency staff in supervising students and coordinating their efforts with instructors. There are advantages and disadvantages to students and agencies when fieldwork is going on, and the author mentions these to clarify what is desired by agencies and the benefits that can be gained. Other supervisor techniques include the use of directories of ethnic social service agencies, like the one developed earlier as part of the author's grant project, and the instructor/practitioner's guidance of student/staff fieldwork activities. Learning objectives are presented in this section for individuals to develop sensitivity to ethnic communities and to show how instructors/practitioners can advise students/staff in fieldwork projects from start to finish. By developing effective communication at this early phase of doing research in ethnic communities, as well as following proper research ethics, the stage is being set for the development of trust between fieldworker and community members.

In part II, the book goes into the actual fieldwork experience of others and then shows us how ethnic groups and communities are organized. As we look at early ethnographies that were done, one can see that trust becomes an issue to establish through fieldwork practice since it does not occur automatically. Through trial and error, one can see how credibility and trust requires not only good communication but a deeper knowledge of the group one is studying. The book then goes into the nature of communities and how access may be challenging depending on how insular they are. Adapting fieldwork methods to these communities becomes important because it is in this section that the reader can understand the concerns of ethnic members who feel victimized by the researcher and who receive little benefit from the research done on them.

In part III the book focuses on each ethnic community that was studied in the grant project (African American, Lao, Vietnamese Chinese, Vietnamese, Japanese American, Mexican American, and Samoan) and highlights the ethnic group's views of research and the interview process. It is possible to see the dynamics of culture at work in their responses and the author comments on their statements to enrich this data. By presenting the views of ethnic members in this way, it becomes possible for the reader to know how to approach ethnic members appropriately, how to behave around them, and how to respect their worth as research subjects.

In part IV, the final chapter of the book, a theoretical framework for building trust is presented, as well as specific fieldwork recommendations for each ethnic group. This information should be especially helpful to individuals who are unfamiliar with the ethnic group's cultural norms and values. They are part of the basic thrust of this book that fieldwork cannot proceed without the building of trust. Trust or the lack of trust determines how much information is acquired from groups, how much interaction is allowed, and how much honesty prevails in the interaction between outsider and insider.

The reader may be wondering why the title of this book is about building trust. The need to build trust implies that it isn't there, as though something is missing in a relationship, or worse, that there is negativity conducive to prejudice and discrimination. This was not supposed to be a book on prejudice and discrimination, but these things can certainly be an ongoing historical presence that does not go away that easily.

On a personal note, the author has read a lot about the subject of race relations and prejudice/discrimination. She knows the theories as a sociologist and, as a psychotherapist, she can go into the treatment of some of these issues. What she has not found from the readings yet is a way to bring about large-scale change in the negativity so that building trust is not an issue any more between people of different racial and ethnic backgrounds. Why is this important to her? Maybe it is because she is much older now and needs to know what it is that we have not learned as a society. Maybe she is still haunted by the experience of seeing a group of African American college students get pulled over in their car and frisked by Los Angeles police, not because they were doing anything wrong, but because of their skin color. The driver also got a ticket for a headlight that was out, but not before the policeman searched the car and looked under the hood. The author wasn't acting as a sociologist when she observed this scene. She was following the students to a home party in Los Angeles after they had all attended a scholarship banquet on campus.

Theoretically, building trust is not just a key factor in doing good field studies. It would be a basic element in reducing prejudice and discrimination. LaPiere had the observational data to show that contact reduces prejudice, which in turn could reduce discrimination, but he did not explore the process by which negative beliefs can change and be substituted by more positive beliefs about people. This would be important in the reduction of prejudice and discrimination.

In this book, the idea of building trust will be treated as a process that can culminate in positive beliefs toward other groups. Because a theoretical framework has not yet been developed around trust as a reducer of prejudice and discrimination, this book will attempt to make inroads in this direction.

Using the data collected earlier, and insights from other theoretical studies, the last chapter will address the issue of trust in greater detail, with the hope of building a theory that helps us understand what we have not done, what we could do, and what some of us are already doing. If this book does guide others in some small way toward a reduction in negative group interaction, then it has more than accomplished its purpose.

*Part I*

This section begins with basic guidelines for doing fieldwork that can be found in methodology textbooks in sociology and anthropology. Though the content may appear familiar, the sentiment is different and is more about tuning in to people than about learning fieldwork techniques accurately. This approach is taken because the author is exploring the issue of trust and how a social-environmental context can be created that will encourage the building of trust. If this can be done way before there is contact between people of different ethnic/racial backgrounds, then trust would be much easier to maintain once contact is made.

In chapter 3: Supervision and the Ethics of Doing Fieldwork, we continue with building up an environment conducive to trust, only now we have taken the learning experience out to the community and the agencies who serve ethnic members. Instead of just focusing on the practice of agency supervision, this chapter gets into the need for the kind of communication between the fieldwork student (or instructor) and the agency that goes beyond just setting up a basic contract for fieldwork. Expectations must be clearly communicated and there must be a good fit between the agency and the placement person. This is, of course, true for fieldwork success in any neighborhood, but it becomes more urgent in ethnic communities because of the greater likelihood of divergence between fieldworker and community members in cultural values and trust.

The section on fieldwork ethics goes deeper into the need for shared expectations as it looks at the ways that poor communication can lead to violations of privacy, exploitation and harm, and negative consequences for future research. When ethnic members are not properly informed of the nature of the research and how it will affect their community, then they can feel used or exploited. When researchers do not properly understand cultural taboos, they can violate the ethnic person or community's privacy. Good communication is essential to maintaining fieldwork ethics that will minimize distrust and build up trust in an ethnic community.

*Chapter 2*

# Basic Guidelines for Doing Fieldwork

Anyone living in a multicultural environment could benefit from learning about ethnic groups no matter what kind of work he or she does. If individuals don't have an understanding of the populations they serve and interact with, then misunderstandings can occur. Whether these populations are patients, clients, or research respondents, they are often members of ethnic groups, and understanding their cultural differences and unique historical experiences becomes important in providing them with the best possible services. For example, there is a shortage of minorities in the health professions in general so that most clients are not being served by those who understand their culture. Culture profoundly influences diagnosis, treatment, and responsiveness to health care workers, so this makes it critical for educators in this field and others to train practitioners in cross-cultural care (Johnson & Smith 2002, 28–29).

Since our students will eventually be working in the community in professions that will bring them face to face with many ethnic members, it is critical for educators to provide them with the necessary tools to make their jobs easier as they interact with ethnic members. The techniques of fieldwork in ethnic communities are one of these tools. A way to do this is to have a course that deals with people or a way to study people that includes an ethnic component. Courses that already deal with ethnic content could include a fieldwork component. According to Paul Chikahisa, methodology courses especially should integrate minority content into their curriculum so that it is infused with relevant minority issues and problems (Chikahisa et al. 1976). Since these courses are studying people in their natural environment, like surveys done in African American neighborhoods, students should learn about these people and communities first and develop an awareness of cultural variations. After this is done, they could benefit from research techniques specific to ethnic communities.

Since there are many disciplines that train students to serve populations in our society, this chapter and the ones that follow hopefully can be adapted to fit these discipline's needs. For example, social workers serve minority groups and immigrant populations as they attempt to match up community services with client needs. Human Service workers staff agencies that provide vital services to diverse populations. Nurses, doctors, and medical practitioners see patients from all walks of life and from many different ethnic cultures. Their understanding of the patient's culture can improve patient compliance with medical regimens and also help them provide the most appropriate services for the patient. Mental health workers including psychiatrists, psychologists, and marriage and family therapists work with ethnic clients that have both relationship difficulties and mental health symptoms. An understanding of the client's culture is the basic context for developing treatment plans.

All of these disciplines can benefit from an understanding of fieldwork procedures, so this chapter provides basic guidelines in as simple a way as possible. Sociology and anthropology students will be familiar with these guidelines through their disciplines. Instructors in other fields or agency workers can acquire a basic knowledge of fieldwork that can be used to train others such as staff or students. As these guidelines are learned, it will be possible to apply them to ethnic groups and to see how they may lead to building trust, which is the main thesis of this book.

As a first step, instructors can guide students in developing sensitivity to people as they use research tools in ethnic communities. The following student learning objectives might be helpful in this regard. They were developed over the years by those in the field of social work and are included in a fieldwork manual developed by the USC School of Social Work (1979). They are broadened here to include an understanding of ethnic groups.

## STUDENT LEARNING OBJECTIVES

The following objectives are skills that the student should be acquiring when doing fieldwork in ethnic communities:

1. Awareness of his/her own learning pattern
2. Acceptance of the role of being a student in paraprofessional work
3. Ability to work with the supervisor or instructor to identify types of learning experiences needed
4. Willingness to try new experiences and/or adapt to the ethnic culture of other groups

5. Acceptance of areas or lack of competency and knowledge (knowing how little you know of other groups and using this awareness as an incentive for gaining knowledge about them)
6. Ability to incorporate new intellectual knowledge into one's own attitude, so that it can be broadened through contact with ethnic groups
7. Ability to relate intuitive skills to concepts and principles of fieldwork methodology
8. Recognition of the need to relate the fieldwork experience to academic courses and to apply discipline ideas to fieldwork practice (i.e., using the theory from ethnic minority courses when out in the community and using community experiences to understand theory)
9. Ability to make use of such personal attributes as objectivity, understanding, patience, respect for the rights of others, imagination, sensitivity, warmth and receptivity to clients and respondents
10. Ability to become involved in interaction with others
11. Ability to learn from past experiences
12. Ability to treat respondents as individuals—respecting their self-worth, accepting them as they are, having empathy for their problems, having nonjudgmental attitudes toward them, moving at their pace, and starting where they are
13. Skill in both verbal and nonverbal communication; this includes the ability to listen and respond honestly and appropriately
14. Knowledge of the internal organizational structure of the agency or community; this includes learning about client-respondent roles and responsibilities, lines of authority, and channels of communication for decision-making

When instructors incorporate ethnic community fieldwork into their courses, these objectives can be very useful. Instructors may also wish to venture out into the field before teaching class to acquire fieldwork knowledge, if they do not have it already. The thing to keep in mind is that an instructor cannot teach only research techniques or skills to students, which is commonly done in university courses, or the substantive knowledge or theory of ethnic groups that helps students formulate problems. There is a human dimension missing that is needed to help students develop the right attitude for working with people.[1]

A fieldwork methodology course will usually emphasize the teaching of practical skills for community data collection. The research skills combined with the formulation of a theoretical problem will form the basis for the student going out into the community to do his study. However, what the instructor usually fails to include in his course is a topic on developing proper attitudes toward people and especially those of another culture. Perhaps this is a difficult thing to teach, but it is sorely needed because the student will be in constant interaction with community members. In most cases he will learn, on his own, how to behave around the people he will study, but the instructor, through meetings, can supervise this direct and intensive learning experience of the student so that he can constantly assess his values. Value and attitude change occur through a gradual process of learning, but once it occurs, the student should find it most useful.

As one can see, this awareness of ethnic members goes beyond the development of communication skills or the learning of interview techniques. It implies going into a community and accepting the people as they are without attempting to change their behavior and practices in line with expectations that are not those of the community. For example, many people do research in a community in the name of social reform or because they want to help people. Usually, these researchers fail to make progress with people because their value system is diametrically opposed to that of the individuals they are trying to help.

In order to avoid this problem, students need to constantly assess their own values throughout the fieldwork period. Only then will they be able to respect community members for who they are and acquire their cooperation. Students may go into the human services for a variety of reasons, but they need to learn that there are certain ways of working in the community that are more effective than others. The list of student learning objectives mentioned above points out some of the ways to avoid developing attitudes that are patronizing to ethnic community members. The list is not exhaustive, and an instructor could probably spend a whole semester developing ideas on how to interact with ethnic members. However, it is a start in learning how to treat community members as unique human beings and to avoid the use of labels that are offensive to them.

## MAINTAINING INSTRUCTOR-STUDENT INTERACTION

The instructor should be working with the student to supervise his activities in the community and to advise him in those areas where fieldwork difficulties arise. In order to maintain an ongoing relationship with the student, it is important that instructors develop some type of system that insures contact and communication between themselves and the student. The following is a brief list of ideas on how this can be accomplished.

1. In the early stages of fieldwork, acquire personal information about the student that will enable you to have a biographical sketch of him. This can be accomplished either through an interview with the student or by obtaining a written essay from him on the following things: his interests, attitudes about himself, experiences, pattern of learning, motivation, and use of self. This biographical information can be used by the instructor to

help the student adapt to the fieldwork situation he is in and to assess the student's values as he is learning.

Another way to acquire information about the student is to have him write a paper on what he hopes to accomplish out in the field. This is designed to see the way the student thinks. If he has a desire to reform people, the instructor could work with him on this and try to bring about a shift in perspective. The information from this paper will be useful in advising and in helping students deal with their attitudes.

A third idea of a similar nature is to have the student do a critique of a certain article dealing with a theme or issue, such as child-rearing practices. Have the student review an article or draw up a hypothetical example that can be critiqued. The critique will reveal the student's way of thinking and his attitudes, which the supervisor can then discuss with him.

2. Have students keep a detailed fieldwork log describing their experiences at the fieldwork site. This log can be used for a number of purposes, that is, assisting the learning of the student throughout the fieldwork experience, as a source of topics for discussion with the student, for advising purposes, and as a way of noting the progress of the student. In place of a log, students could be asked to write up narrative descriptions of their assignments and experiences.

    Another method, perhaps to supplement the log, is to have a checklist of things the student should be looking for while doing fieldwork. These things would be items relevant to the area of study, but they could also include such things as fieldtrips; attending agency meetings and conferences; interviewing individuals, families, and various groups in the community; doing administrative work or consultation at an agency; and attending cultural activities in the community.

3. Have a conference with the student periodically to disseminate relevant materials, provide information about the community, and provide basic fieldwork instruction. (This could be done at the beginning, middle, and end of the fieldwork period.) The final conference should identify the knowledge, values, and practice skills that the student has achieved. Any further need for study or more fieldwork practice should be pointed out by the instructor at this point.

## STEP-BY-STEP PROCEDURES FOR DOING FIELDWORK[2]

This section will cover general guidelines and information that will be of help to any student who plans to do fieldwork in an ethnic community. The instructor plays an important role as advisor to the student because it is his responsibility to make sure that the student has some understanding of this material. The advisor should also have a thorough knowledge of the selected community or at least be able to introduce the student to someone who does have this experience. This other person, or persons, could be faculty or non-faculty members who are knowledgeable and reliable. Having the proper advisory supervision is of the utmost importance for a student who is in the initial stages of developing a research project.

## General Guidelines

1. Choosing a Location

   The student should, if possible, visit the ethnic community he intends to examine for his study, or several of them, to develop a sense of familiarity with it and to help him make a final selection for a study. At the same time he is doing this, he should begin preliminary reading and eventually narrow down his choice of ideas to a community and a specific problem to investigate.

2. Developing a Research Proposal

   After a problem has been defined, the student should prepare a research proposal with the guidance of his advisor. With the exception of cases where the student has had experience working with that particular topic, the research proposal should be considered a pilot study. The proposal should contain the following: a short description of the problem, a thorough review of literature, methods for accomplishing the research, a budget and timeline for the study, and tentative hypotheses to be investigated. The form of research proposals varies somewhat from field-to-field in the social sciences, but these points are usually found in most formats used by different disciplines. It is particularly important that the student exhausts the literature on the problem and that he have a basic understanding of the methodology necessary to give validity to the study. The advisor should help the student find appropriate literature in the library and make sure he selects a simple methodology that will allow him to get at least preliminary results.

   It is also wise to build in some flexibility in a preliminary research design, because what usually happens in practice is that the original problem is either found to be insignificant, or it is not possible to study it. Flexibility allows the student to shift to the important problem as it gets revealed on the fieldwork scene or to another related aspect of it if there is difficulty in studying this problem.

3. Assembling Equipment

   Before leaving for the field, all of the required clothing and equipment should be assembled. This is not much of a problem if the student is working near home, but it can be of great importance if the community is far away and isolated. In general, it is a good rule to keep equipment down to a minimum on a first venture, perhaps a camera and a small tape recorder being the only things taken. Videotaping is more difficult and should not be attempted by a novice fieldworker. The advisor should be alert to the practicality of having certain equipment out in the field and, if possible, introduce the student to someone in the community who will help him with necessary items until he gets adjusted to the customs of the people.

4. Curriculum

   In social science fieldwork it is also necessary for the student to have had certain basic courses so that the concepts involved in doing this type of research are not totally foreign to him. He should have some understanding of how research is conducted in his particular discipline, the current theories employed, and how to use discipline tools in practical application. It is the advisor's responsibility to determine the student's proficiency in these areas and recommend appropriate courses. Students should also have some rudimentary knowledge of the language of the ethnic group to be studied.

5. Group Projects

   If at all possible, the advisor should help the student get involved in multidisciplinary group projects involving research in the ethnic community. With such projects the infrastructure is already set up to help the student learn about the community in general and to know what to expect. This approach to fieldwork is particularly valuable if the community is distant or very different from what the student is accustomed to seeing. In addition, these projects usually include seminars and specific classes, which will help the student complete his research proposal, gather the correct equipment, and learn more about the community. Such a project also provides contact with other people from the United States, which is important if the student is planning a lengthy stay out of the country. In any case, the advisor must make sure that the student has permission to carry out his research from the host government and/or community.

## Guiding the Work of the Student during the Actual Fieldwork

Once the student actually enters the field, it is extremely important that he be closely supervised. It is best if he has access to the advisor at all times, but this is possible only if the student is working in a community close to the university, if he is on a project, or if the advisor is simultaneously in the field. The novice student is advised to undertake fieldwork in one of these three situations.

The first few days, after the student has arrived on the scene, are very important in the development of the study. A student should have letters of introduction or should be introduced to the community authorities by an informant and/or his advisor. The advisor should also inform the student of any necessary precautions to take to safeguard his health, particularly if the sanitary conditions are bad. The climate and food may be very different in the field community from what the student is accustomed to, and the first few days can be quite important in establishing a pattern that will allow him to conduct his study free of illness.

It is also at this time that the student will have his first experiences with the ethnocentric beliefs and customs of the group he is studying, which may be emotionally trying for him. He should follow the recommendations of the advisor to insure a receptive fieldwork environment. However, the advisor should attempt to "read" students' strengths and weaknesses before sending them out into the field. Some individuals are simply not suited to the rigors of overseas fieldwork or they have values that are not amenable to working in certain communities. Students should be carefully channeled into research areas where they have a reasonable chance of succeeding.

If the advisor does not know any local people who can help the student to find housing and aid him in making contacts, local government officials or agencies can perform this function. It is very important that the student have the assistance of people he knows when he begins his study. They can help him to avoid unacceptable behavior around community members and be of great help in locating the precise area where the study is to be carried out. Some fairly simple tasks that will allow students to get a feel for the community are the following: choosing a sample, making a map, doing an inventory of certain types of structures or material items. By the time this work is completed, the student will begin to know the area and people a little better and will probably make some connections that will enable him to begin his actual study.

After the student begins to collect data for the problem he has chosen, it is important that he meet regularly, at least once a week, with his advisor. This enables the advisor to monitor the student's progress and to make sure that valuable insights are brought into focus and developed further. Also, the advisor can spot unproductive endeavors and direct the research along more fruitful lines. Speaking regularly with an experienced fieldwork advisor can also alleviate some of the anxieties of novice students.

At these weekly meetings, the advisor should make sure that the student is keeping an up-to-date and complete set of field notes. In anthropology, notes are usually taken by using G. P. Murdock's, *Outline of Cultural Materials*, which is a topical guide for arranging all types of cultural materials.

Students should have this with them in the field. While they are in the field, it is to the student's advantage to type up field notes every night. This helps the advisor to run quickly through his notes and make sure that all is going well and to quickly detect anything of unusual interest that may have gone unnoticed by the student. In addition, it helps to keep the student's materials orderly.

## Handling Difficult Situations in Ethnic Communities

There are many things that can go wrong when students are doing fieldwork in an ethnic community. They can inadvertently bring hostility on themselves or, in other instances, be made a scapegoat for local ills. If the situation is grave and possibly life-threatening, the advisor must tell the student to leave. Hopefully, there is at least enough flexibility in the research proposal for another community to be considered for the investigation of the problem. In other cases, the student may realize that it is all right to stay, but the original research problem must be changed. This may be because the topic is a very sensitive one and data is very difficult or impossible to collect. If the asking of questions brings out the hostility of the local people, the student is wise to select a more neutral research problem.

Usually, there are numerous other smaller problems that come up on a day-to-day basis when fieldwork is done, and anthropology has developed some general rules to deal with them. For example, the cardinal rule of the anthropological fieldworker is: "don't mess up so bad that nobody can ever work in the community again." If a student finds that he just cannot adapt to local customs, then he should realize that he has not found his proper spot and try to locate another community to study and possibly even another ethnic group. Students about to embark upon fieldwork are advised to stay clear of community and national politics and to avoid sexual involvements with local people.

There is also the problem of wanting to do research on taboo subjects. This should probably not be attempted by a beginning fieldworker. Even if he surreptitiously gathers data on sacred items, deviant sexual practices, or crimes he has observed, it may violate ethical canons to publish such material. If the student discovers that the local people are being exploited by the larger government and wants to make this known publicly, he runs the risk of having his fieldwork terminated. This, of course, involves personal choice and sometimes presents a degree of risk to the researcher. Advisors should point this out and try to steer the student clear of such controversial domains, at least during his initial experience. In general, if research results cannot be freely published, the study should not be undertaken.

Sometimes there are difficulties when the chosen ethnic group does not want to be studied. This frequently happens with American Indians who feel that they have suffered enough exploitation by social scientists in the past. For beginners, it is probably best if they work with people who are not hostile or seriously opposed to having a student researcher in their midst. In general, though, the student should be aware if serious difficulties will arise for him or for individuals in the ethnic group as a result of information collected. The advisor should help to weed out this data so that the student researcher maintains his responsibility to those he studies.

## Utilization of Resources and Reference Materials

Use of reference material is very important in the initial stages of developing a research proposal. The most effective way to define a significant problem is to read up on the general subject, or about a specific ethnic group, and identify particular areas of interest or relevance. The next step is to find out what needs to be done or discovered regarding this area of interest. Library resources are important, but talking to people in agencies or at community facilities is also quite helpful. Agencies often need volunteers, and this provides a useful means of entrance to the ethnic group. By serving an agency, a student can learn about the community while he begins to realize significant research possibilities. The agency or community facility can also perform a supervisory role and provide the infrastructure within which the research can be carried out (See chapter 3). Using a directory of ethnic agencies and facilities will be helpful in giving the student a reference point for finding out about those community services in which he can participate.

While the student is actually conducting his research, agency personnel can fulfill the role of field advisor or help to supplement that role if someone else is doing it. Members of these institutions are usually quite knowledgeable regarding the day-to-day life of the ethnic group. They may also serve as consultants on research projects. It is possible that a research proposal is developed that fits in with the overall work of an agency, and its staff may help the student to publish his results. Participating in a community facility is valuable because the student is able to feel like he is part of a group.

## The Advisor Role in Ethnic Communities

If the advisor is head of a project in which there are a number of other faculty and students involved, he could make each piece of research fit in with an overall research plan, and both faculty and students could work together to achieve specific and general research goals.

Or, the advisor may have been working with a particular ethnic group or set of groups and can help students to develop research proposals that are complementary to his. The advisor would then already know people in the community and would be better able to place students in situations where they would be able to do fieldwork. He may also introduce students to potential informants (individuals of that community and ethnic group who provide information about their group and facilitate the research).

Advisors can participate in the ethnic community with students by accompanying them to the fieldwork site. They may go with the student to meet individuals, to visit agencies and facilities, or merely to investigate possible research locations. People from the community may be encouraged by the advisor to come to the campus to attend seminars, give talks, or be interviewed (for example, for oral history projects). A common data bank could be established that all the members of a class, seminar, or project could use.

Advisors and students may also be invited by community members to fulfill certain roles in the community. For example, both may be called upon to do community labor service, such as weeding the cemetery. They may also participate in rituals and social activities when invited. These two roles are very important in establishing good relations with the members of the community. The advisor may also have contact with various agencies or community facilities and provide student volunteers for some types of work. This can give students an opportunity to acquire data while actually performing a needed function for the ethnic group. In this way, community members are less likely to feel exploited by university workers.

If any difficulties arise between the student and members of the ethnic group, the advisor should try to resolve them. A responsible advisor does his best to place beginning students in a fieldwork situation where people are somewhat flexible and tolerant to the behavior of outsiders.

## Helping Students Implement Their Research Ideas in the Ethnic Community

The most difficult problem a beginning student has in doing fieldwork is finding a place where he can comfortably carry out the proposed plan for research. The most frequently asked question by students is, "How do I get in?" It is very important for the advisor to help his students meet the local people, agency staff, and/or community members so that the student can discuss his ideas and get suggestions as to the best place to conduct his research. Choosing an inappropriate location or failing to contact the necessary authorities can doom a student's research before it gets started. The advisor should have the requisite local authorities identified and letters of introduction prepared before sending a student into the field.

It is possible that the student's research may either be of interest to the community or bring about positive benefits to the community. If this is true, then members of the community may ask the student to help them get a project started and participate in its functioning. For example, a student with a research proposal designed to study how to reduce gang violence may be asked to advise or participate in an ongoing community project with the same goals. The advisor may also put the student in touch with community members working in the same area of research as he is. Because the research would benefit the community, any publications resulting from the study should be made available to local community libraries, offices, and perhaps specific individuals who were instrumental in helping the student conduct his study.

Another area where the advisor can help the student is in obtaining money for implementing his research. This may involve travel and living expenses or funds necessary for carrying out some facet of the proposal. If there is a project going on, some funds from it may be given to the student for his research. In addition, the advisor may introduce the student to community people who are willing to provide funds for carrying out the student's research goals.

The advisor may also help the student convince agencies or facilities to adopt the beneficial results of research. In this way, community members who are struggling with a variety of problems may actually utilize student research proposals. The research conducted by an outsider may provide a needed objective viewpoint, and the advisor could assist the student in finding an opportunity where research results can be discussed.

## Implementing Curriculum Materials in the Fieldwork Situation

Students should take courses both on how to do fieldwork and on the subject of ethnic groups. Once they have chosen a particular ethnic group to study, they should take a course dealing with that group, if possible, and another course on the language of these people. All of this should be done prior to the student's entering the field. During the actual fieldwork stage, it is very helpful if the student can attend more advanced seminars on fieldwork methodology, language study, and the culture of the specific group. In this way the student can apply what he is learning in class directly to the fieldwork situation.

Usually, when an anthropology student goes into the field, he takes G. P. Murdock's *Outline of Cultural Materials*, Pertti Pelto's *Anthropological*

*Research: The Structure of Inquiry*, books on the relevant group, and his research proposal. The proposal will be revised as his fieldwork progresses. He will begin to implement some aspect of methodology that has been learned in class such as participant observation, key-informant interviewing, structured interviews, TAT test, or the case study. These methods may be preferable to actually taking a random sample and applying statistical measures to it, which is somewhat more challenging to do in the field than it is in the classroom.

The student must select the methodological tool or tools that will give him the greatest possibility of producing successful results, but the method must be one that can be applied. Interview schedules are the best technique for survey-type research, but if people refuse to let people in their homes, questionnaires, which can be mailed, may be necessary. At times the interview schedule, questionnaire, or picture TAT tests may be developed in the class and then used in the fieldwork situation. Students may also make use of other skills learned in the university such as photography, folklore collection, or videos.

Specific manuals developed as part of the curriculum or a specific project may be of great use to the student who is just beginning to do fieldwork. These may deal with how to do fieldwork, how to handle difficult situations, or how to do methodology and sampling. Sometimes manuals are developed in class by students and advisors to deal with specific situations.

The student should also have some idea of the current theories in his field and be able to relate them to the data being collected. Thus, a course on anthropological or sociological theory would be essential. Most of the application of the theory will come after the period of fieldwork is over and the student begins writing up his data, but it is very important that he have some knowledge of theory to guide the research during all its stages. In addition, students may be taught how to keep a daily journal of mundane events. In this way they will have a running narrative of things that have occurred to supplement the more formal set of field notes that categorizes material.

## INCORPORATING MINORITY CONTENT INTO COURSES

There are a number of ways to include ethnic content and fieldwork activity in a university course. The approaches and methods will vary depending on the creativity of instructors and the objectives they are trying to achieve for the course. A partial list of ideas is provided below that are based on some of the suggestions made by the faculty trainees of the Pilot Ethnic Research Training Project.

1. Lecturing on cultural variables of the community and pointing out non-verbal characteristics of the ethnic group. Making students aware, through these lectures, of their own nonverbal characteristics and cultural biases.
2. Making available to students a set of ethnic-cultural materials that could be placed in the campus library or kept in the classroom for loaning and reference purposes. These materials could be case studies done by field-workers in anthropology or sociology, or they could be the students' own collected works based on their community experiences.
3. Having role-playing sessions on how to interview members from ethnic communities. The students would not only acquire interviewing skills from this experience but would become aware of the attitudes of ethnic respondents as well. Ethnic members from the community could be brought in to participate in the role-playing so that students will be better able to understand their point of view.
4. Assigning projects to students where they would go out into the ethnic community and do observations or participant observation. The following are examples: doing a mini-ethnography on some topic related to the needs and interests of ethnic members, helping to develop a community program, putting in fieldwork hours at an ethnic agency, and doing a survey of community attitudes on some problem or issue.

The basic reason for incorporating ethnic content into courses is to provide students with a broader foundation for understanding course subject matter and appreciating the dynamics of ethnic life. To accomplish this, it is necessary for the student to have an opportunity to interact with community members. This is not simply a matter of having ethnic members come into class as guest speakers or workshop coordinators. Students must go out into the community to see how life is "out there." Only in this way will they be able to catch ethnic members behaving spontaneously in their natural setting.

## NOTES

1. The author is indebted to Paul Chikahisa for his assistance in developing this section. Mr. Chikahisa was a field instructor at the Asian American Community Mental Health Training Center in Los Angeles in the 1970s and 1980s.

2. The author gratefully acknowledges the assistance of Dr. Sandra Orellana, professor of anthropology, California State University–Dominguez Hills, in developing this section.

## Chapter 3

# Supervision and the Ethics of Doing Fieldwork

Supervision can mean different things to people depending on what field they are in and how the concept is being used. It can mean a type of surveillance that goes on in industries to make sure employees are doing their job, or it can mean a type of training and guidance that helps a person learn certain skills or types of knowledge. In such areas as social work, human services, health sciences, counseling, and the social sciences, it is not unusual to think of supervision as part of a practicum course or an internship whereby an agency is responsible mainly for seeing that a student puts in so many hours of work for a specific amount of academic credit.

Supervision and fieldwork are becoming of increasing importance to academic programs and health care practitioners as neighborhoods become more ethnically diverse. According to Bonder, practitioners need to develop cultural competence so that they can respond adequately to the needs of each client. This includes an ability to gather culturally influenced information, knowing how to interpret it appropriate to the individual's situation, and being able to incorporate it into interventions (Bonder, Martin, and Miracle 2001, 37). This means that students need some exposure to the community people with whom they will be working once they graduate from universities, and it is important that they have some preparation in dealing with these people before starting their professional careers. The experience of doing fieldwork, though, has varied quite a bit depending on the discipline one is in. Some disciplines, like the human services and social work, will have a very elaborate system of fieldwork supervision with agency personnel or field instructors having major responsibility for guiding the student's work.

In other areas, like anthropology, one finds much less supervision when the student first goes out into a community. This seems unusual because anthropology is a field that deals with the study of ethnic cultures—many of which are quite "foreign" to the student—and one would think that the novice would find it intimidating and uncomfortable to venture out alone into new territory. Yet, as Junker points out, the beginning ethnographer can get little guidance from others and enters into something like:

> [A] darkened labyrinth, a social maze through which the field worker must "feel his way." His general adaptation, or his adoption of a role that suits most occasions, grows from a multitude of trial-and-error attempts to improve his opportunities to learn more. He undergoes a more or less profound "sea change" in himself, and whether for better or worse becomes unlike other men, for he has lived in at least two worlds (Junker 1960, 70).

Such a rude awakening seems a little extreme if the novice must "go it alone." Of course there are manuals and books on fieldwork techniques and strategies to instruct him along the way, but they are not the same as having an experienced person along to provide guidance. This became obvious to the author as she attempted to supervise faculty trainees to do fieldwork in ethnic communities. The learning and awareness of the trainees seemed to take longer when they were not given assistance from someone knowledgeable about the culture. Without this guidance, it was also possible for many of them to end up unaware of important cultural variables in the community.

The novice fieldworker who must find his own way may have a different experience of learning. Because he does not have a supervisor in the community or have any friends there, he will oftentimes spend weeks or months trying to involve himself in various kinds of social relationships, as well as trying his hardest to find persons who will advise him, assist him, introduce him, or "go around with him" (Wax 1971, 17). If this is part of a learning experience, it may work out fine if the student has a number of years he can spend just on one field project, for example, a dissertation. However, students doing work for a class assignment will find that they don't have time to learn how to make contacts with informants, get along with community people, and then get insights into cultural meanings and behaviors. For this reason, it may be advantageous to have a supervisory system that will shorten the period of trial-and-error for the student.

The concept of supervision, as used in this book, incorporates a set of fieldwork guidelines to enable the student to develop skills in interacting with people and acquiring knowledge. These guidelines can fit under three types of supervision. They are: general knowledge and information assistance, faculty or instructor guidance, and agency direction or guidance. The author prefers to think of supervision as a means of training and guiding individuals in a direction in which they can acquire knowledge and skills.

What is not implied in this definition is a relationship between student and supervisor whereby one person is in a position of authority over the other and therefore exerts a watchdog function. Supervision facilitates the process by which one gains assistance in a field of endeavor through the resources of another. The supervisor could be thought of as an advisor, a consultant, a mentor, or a teacher presiding over a student or intern's fieldwork activities. This chapter will describe these types of supervision to show how data collection and doing fieldwork can at times be problematic and even lead to distrust.

## GENERAL SUPERVISION

In this type of supervision, the assistance provided is on helping the fieldworker acquire general knowledge and information. The author is referring to a learning process by which a set of rules or guidelines is provided to warn students or fieldworkers of dangers and to advise them in the proper way to proceed in fieldwork activities. This book could partly be used as a supervision instrument because it provides these types of rules or guidelines in a number of areas related to ethnic communities. Other textbooks, such as Williams' *Field Methods in the Study of Culture* (1967), could also be thought of as a supervisory instrument because it is providing beginning-to-end instructions on how to do anthropological fieldwork. Either an agency person, an instructor, or a friend could make these resources known to the student fieldworker, but the supervision comes not so much from someone standing over one's head as it does from someone going over the information with the fieldworker once the acquisition of resources has taken place.

## INSTRUCTOR SUPERVISION

This type of supervision could include any number of activities such as regular consultation with students, advising on interview questions, referring students to agencies, or placing them at a fieldwork site, or observing the student's work at an agency or a community site. What it should involve is the faculty member's careful guidance and direction of the student's entire fieldwork experience. Unfortunately, this does not always happen. In university classes where fieldwork is a part of a lecture course, there is a tendency for the instructor to do minimal supervision of the student's fieldwork activities. The situation may be different at an agency like the one the author visited during the 1980s to observe its training program.

At the Asian American Community Mental Health Training Center in Los Angeles, there was a field instructor who spent his hours actively supervising students. His instruction was geared toward the fieldwork experience, and he kept a close check on what the student was learning. This type of supervision is extremely important, because the student is going out into a community that may be completely new to him in terms of types of people there, patterns of behavior and attitudes that exist, and cultural beliefs and traditions. A valuable part of the fieldwork experience would be for the student to learn to look with the eyes of the community members and to hear with their ears.

In later sections of this book, there will be many pages devoted to the perspective of ethnic members and the nature of ethnic communities, which should be useful to the student. As far as the instructor's role is concerned, there is a need for supervision to be active rather than passive. The instructor should accompany the student out into the community as much as possible and point out things to him/her that will facilitate the individual's path to cultural learning.

## AGENCY SUPERVISION

So far, agencies have been getting stuck with the brunt of student supervision. This is because students work under their jurisdiction and within facilities that may be far removed from campuses. Agency supervision depends on such things as adequate staffing and the availability of fieldwork activities appropriate for the student. It usually involves directing activities of students as they fall in line with the normal operations of the agency. These activities could involve such things as volunteer counseling, clerical assistance, program development, survey work, home visitations, tutoring/teaching in such areas as English as a second language, and learning skills of various types. These agencies may be in ethnic communities already so the student is experiencing the community through working at the agency. In cases where the staff is not of the same ethnic group as the clients they serve, there would be a need for the agencies to have supervisors over these staff members. Their task would be to have these individuals achieve cultural competence through the effective gathering of information, through identifying goals for treatment or service, and providing interventions that reflect the client's cultural as well as service needs (Bonder, Martin, and Miracle 2001, 39).

In the following sections, a number of supervision styles will be presented as seen in agencies. There is no one prescription of how agencies should supervise since they vary so much in function and responsibilities. The main concern is that they are able to work with instructors in providing the best possible learning experience for students. Like the instructor, an agency staff member will be overburdened by other duties, but, through their cooperative efforts, it is possible for arrangements to be made so that each assists the other.

## Agency Needs and Supervision

As part of the Pilot Ethnic Research Project, a number of ethnic community agency directors were contacted to find out how they felt about supervising students and the type of supervision they would be able to provide at their agency. They were also asked to provide information on the advantages and disadvantages of having students do fieldwork at their agency, their expectations for fieldwork students, and their expected relationship with the student's instructor. The following information provides a description of some of the needs and expectations of agencies, as well as identifying some of the supervisory techniques those agencies have developed for students who come to their agency for fieldwork experiences.

The type of supervision that an agency does will depend on a number of factors. These include the size of the staff, the type of programs and services offered by the agency, the quality and type of supervision required by agencies, and other resources available to the agency. The following examples of fieldwork supervision were mentioned by agencies based on their own peculiar needs and circumstances.

*Minimum Supervision.* In one case, minimum supervision was all the agency could handle because of a shortage of staff. Students had to be qualified volunteers who knew about the agency service and could function with little supervision from the staff. More supervision could take place only if funding sources were found to increase agency personnel. In another case, minimum supervision was all that was needed because of the types of services offered. The students would simply participate with agency fieldworkers and do observations while program coordinators would supervise the students. Sometimes an agency may have few staff members to supervise students, but the students are welcome because they free up the personnel to work on other things such as providing more service opportunities.

*Maximum Supervision.* This is more often provided in an internship or training program for students who are learning a variety of skills. Maximum supervision is needed in programs that require diligent and specialized knowledge such as in social work, or marriage and family therapy.

*Close Supervision.* This is usually provided by a knowledgeable staff person such as the director or assistant director of an agency. The main concern here is in keeping the student on the right track of whatever he or she is learning.

When students volunteer at an agency to do fieldwork, there are certain advantages that result from their endeavors. Agencies mentioned the following as advantages for them: students motivate agency clients or act as role models for them (low income or youthful clients especially), the agency director and staff have more time to do important things related to their programs, the agency gains new ideas from students and a new enthusiasm, the agency receives more help in acquiring information about their clients, students help in various programs such as counseling, and they provide a necessary service to the community for the elderly and youth. The advantage to the student is that he or she has an opportunity to learn, first-hand, the needs of ethnic communities. He or she also gains knowledge and research experience through participation on different projects.

Agencies also mentioned a number of factors that could be a disadvantage to them should students do fieldwork at their agency. The following is a summary of these factors.

Some students may not be able to handle the types of clients that agencies receive, that is, drug addicts, alcoholics, and the mentally unstable. They may not have enough experience working with agency services and clients, and sometimes they are very restricted in the amount of time they have at the agency. Some are not highly motivated or interested in the agency work, and others are not qualified; that is, they are not bilingual and cannot work with ethnic clients who speak no English. Some students require a lot of supervision, especially if they are first-time volunteers, and this supervision takes time away from regular staff duties. The major problem, though, is that the student is not at an agency long enough to learn that much about the work and to get to know the community people. This is something agencies consider very important, and it is especially necessary in the case of the Samoan community where the elderly need to be approached gradually before trust and rapport can be built up.

When it comes to preferences for certain kinds of students, many agencies prefer someone who is of a specific ethnic background who has a specific interest or skills of various types and who is bilingual in the language used by most of their clients. One agency preferred a student who is sensitive to inner-city conditions and who is Mexican American, mainly so that he or she could attract more young adults from the Mexican American community in their predominantly African American area. An ability to teach remedial reading to slow learners was also desired. Other agencies preferred a dedicated Asian or American person, a person who is bilingual in Chinese or Vietnamese with ESL-teaching skills, or a person who is Samoan and interested in becoming a social worker.

Once an agency agrees to supervise a student fieldworker, the supervision can involve interaction with the student's instructor. Therefore, agency directors were asked how they would like to meet with instructors. Responses were varied but all involved some type of arrangement that should be made between agency personnel and the instructor to facilitate the sharing of information and to understand the fieldwork assignment. These arrangements included coordinating the fieldwork schedule to meet both student and agency needs, meeting with the instructor, talking to him or her on the phone to establish rapport or develop a close relationship, meeting together to discuss the fieldwork goals, purpose, student objectives and assignments, meeting with the instructor once a semester and seeing a report of the project assignment when the fieldwork is completed, and meeting with the instructor before the semester begins to negotiate a work statement and to inform the instructor of the type of work the agency would have for the student. There may be other agencies, not included in this sample, that prefer to work directly with the student and do very little relating with the instructor.

Supervision is an important component of student fieldwork, but agencies also have certain expectations of the student that go beyond hours put in at the fieldwork site or the performing of routine activities. One agency expected students to be part of the team and to believe in teamwork. A good attitude and enthusiasm were important to this team effort. Other characteristics that agencies expected of students were trustworthiness and reliability. Another director expected the student to be interested in the agency project and not just do the work as a class assignment. It was important that the person be able to relate to existing problems and to have a dedication to social work.

When addressing these agency expectations, the author was thinking about the issue of exploitation. The agency directors were not asked how they felt about this issue, but since it is a problem that can exist, some mention of it should be made. Exploitation can occur by both the agency and the student. Agencies can exploit students who volunteer to work for them, with or without pay, when they are not concerned with what the student learns and just want to use student labor to facilitate their work. Having a student status is not always an advantage in this case because it means that the student can be exploited to the point of abuse. Students can also end up being caught in loyalties to the agency, the instructor, and their own family when their agency work becomes over demanding. This is why it is important to have both the faculty and agency supervise the student's fieldwork, but it is not always clear where the supervision of one ends and the other begins.

Students themselves could be exploiters of the community and agency. For example, in the process of getting a paper done for a class, they may simply jump into the community, use its resources, and jump out again after getting the information they need. They are not really serving the agency in this case; they are simply using agency time and resources and then not showing the

community the results of the research. This makes community members distrust the fieldworker. It is very important for students to learn how to give to
the community while taking from it and to appreciate the community people
and their resources. This requires that they consider much more than just how
to get their paper written. It requires an understanding of fieldwork ethics.


## FIELDWORK ETHICS

Unlike the field of marital and family therapy, ethical concerns in doing
ethnographic fieldwork are not clearly defined or regulated. This does not
mean that they are unimportant. In fact, practicing good fieldwork ethics is
vital to successful and accurate data gathering, and it has a great impact on
building trust.

Because of the importance of this topic, this section of the chapter will
attempt to identify ethical areas that are relevant to working in ethnic communities. These areas will, of course, overlap with the ethics of doing fieldwork
in general. We can start by discussing Hammersley and Atkinson's (1995)
five ethical issues: informed consent, privacy, harm, exploitation, and the
consequences for future research.

Informed consent is loosely applied in fieldwork research, though in the
psychotherapy area it is strictly regulated by State Boards. This concept
means that people who are studied know the specifics of the research project
as it relates to their involvement, and they are agreeing to participate under
these conditions. Normally, there would be a contract that individuals sign
so the researcher is not held liable for any negative consequences to the participants if informed consent is actually put into practice. However, rarely is
this contract used in fieldwork. It would go against the goal of doing covert
research if it were used here and would make it difficult for researchers to
gain entrance into esoteric groups who wish to remain private. A case in
point is Festinger, Riecken, and Schachter's study (1956) of a group of fly-
ing saucer believers whose leader predicted the end of the world. Access to
this group would have been impossible if the motives of the researchers were
known to the group.

Though there may be reasons for doing covert research in ethnic communities, like studying an esoteric subgroup within the community; in
general it would make sense to keep research overt. It is even better when
the researcher can communicate his research goals and ideas clearly to
ethnic community members so that they are well informed of the research
study. Ethnic members know who the outsider is, and a researcher coming in disguised or not disguised may have a difficult time really getting

to know the people and building enough trust to get reliable data. Maybe it is even okay to be different from the group you are studying as long as you are honest, because the goal is to build a relationship through research rather than trying to be "one of the gang." Liebow makes it clear through his retrospective that he was still the outsider, a white man in a black community, even after a year of hanging out at "Tally's Corner" and interacting regularly with the men there (Smith and Kornblum 1989, 35–44). Yet, his ethnography certainly did not suffer from the fact that Liebow let his subjects know who he was and what he was there to study; he was able to complete an insightful fieldwork project in an ethnic community. Though he was never one of the "gang," he was trusted to the extent possible by those who got to know him.

Disclosure of one's research goals, interests, and background would be beneficial to the ethnic community as well as to the researcher. Not only would collaboration be greater when there is openness on the part of the researcher and trust be built up more easily with the community, but the ethnic community would have a greater sense of efficacy over what is happening in their community. This empowerment would reinforce their interest in the research and encourage expression of their viewpoints. Though a formal informed-consent procedure may not be practical in a fieldwork setting, it is a good practice to keep respondents informed and to have their consent in research studies.

Privacy is another ethical issue relevant to the study of ethnic groups. Privacy is a right in the United States, and anyone can maintain this right by simply saying they don't wish to talk about a subject. However, people do not always know what will get published from the responses they make to researchers, and this is how privacy can be invaded. For example, a researcher may find that there is a high rate of domestic violence in an ethnic community based on the responses that individuals have made about it. How this gets written up by the researcher and the way that he presents the data and analyzes it could make the ethnic members feel that their privacy has been violated, especially if domestic violence was not part of the stated purpose of the research.

Privacy is a serious issue when it comes to the violation of cultural taboos and norms. Groups with a traditional ethnic culture would be very upset if tabooed subjects were brought up by the researcher. If the researcher tried to pursue these subjects with the respondents, it would be a violation of their privacy. Taboos are kept secret for a reason. There are cultural norms forbidding the discussion of these topics. When the researcher does not respect the respondent's right to privacy on these subjects, he is violating their trust in him.

When the ethnic group is not so traditional in values and beliefs, it is still possible to find a group who prefers to maintain privacy over a lot of information. African American males are one such group. They are known for not using psychotherapy because they don't want to reveal a lot about themselves. Even when they do show up for mental health counseling, the therapist has to go slow in establishing trust and eliciting personal information.

Though informed consent and privacy are important issues, the possibility of causing harm to individuals that have been studied is the most serious ethical concern in doing fieldwork in ethnic communities. Harm can take place through the publication of research findings that are damaging to the individuals of an ethnic group by affecting their reputation; it can even put people in danger based on the way published research data is used by others (Hammersley and Atkinson 1995). Though ethnographic accounts are published to provide information to a larger audience by a neutral researcher, who is to say that a publication on undocumented Mexicans in a section of Los Angeles won't result in arrests being made and individuals deported back to Mexico? Or what about a study of a Middle Eastern Muslim community in a suburb of a large city? Would this work be used to identify potential terrorists leading to actions that would disrupt the community and create fear in people?

We have little control over the potential harm that can come to people that are studied once a publication gets released. However, we can take measures to minimize risk to individuals as much as possible during the study. One way to do this is to create a fictitious name for the community and to keep the names of participants anonymous. Individuals can also be told what the study will be used for and how it might affect their community. This is tied in to informed consent, but what is more important is to encourage respondents to give feedback on the way they want their community represented through research results.

Exploitation has been mentioned earlier in terms of agencies and student fieldworkers. As a serious ethical concern, it applies to any group of subjects that are being used for the purposes of research and not getting anything back for their effort. A simple solution to this problem is to give respondents some modest compensation for their participation, whether it is $20, an inexpensive gift card, or some recognition for their effort. These forms of compensation can be used in ethnic communities as well, but what is more important is to give back to the community something that will benefit the group in the long run. This would be the ultimate way of preventing exploitation.

Ideally, research should benefit an ethnic community by informing the public of specific needs that the community has or showing how the community has resources that can be used by others. These resources could be as varied as having community knowledge about taking care of elders, having a large youth population that is available for community activities, or having cultural wisdom and knowledge that others could use. Community needs could include medical services for parents, children and elders, employment opportunities for men, women or youth, mental health services, and entrepreneurship development opportunities. When a research study can act as the catalyst for bringing about positive change in a community in a way that serves its people, then it is giving back to the community on a long-term basis.

Even if researchers do not go this far, they can still be a catalyst for the community either as a community activist or a concerned citizen. Kornblum ended up getting really involved in South Chicago politics as he followed the lives of steelworkers in *Blue Collar Community* (1989). Not only did he live in the neighborhood, but he was active in local political campaigns and worked for several months as a subforeman in a steel mill. This involvement made it easier for him to work on changing the community. Of course, many ethnographers have given back to the ethnic community in uncountable hours of service and by their continual presence in the community long after the original research had been done.

The last ethical concern is the consequences for future research. When people are offended by research that was done on their community they are not likely to be receptive to other researchers coming in later on. The ethical obligation here is that the individual ethnographer should not mess things up for other researchers by damaging relationships in the community (Hammersley and Atkinson 1995).

Though researchers may not agree on how serious this ethical concern is, it is very serious when it comes to the study of ethnic members or communities. Ethnic groups are very sensitive about what is written about them, especially if it is negative and ends up stereotyping the group. They will be wary and distrustful of the next researcher who comes along if an earlier study denigrated them in any way. Samoans have been distrustful of research on their community ever since Margaret Mead made them look sexually promiscuous in her early study (1928). These are Samoans who now live in the United States and are later generations of the group she studied; yet, they still know about her book.

One way to prevent negative consequences for future research is to make one's research results or analyses available to community members to review. Their feedback can be useful in modifying the slant or posture of a final document that will have wider dissemination. Accuracy of the document is not necessarily compromised when the community viewpoint is represented in the text.

In summary, fieldwork ethics are very important when studying ethnic communities no matter how acculturated the members are. Each ethical concern discussed here is really about building trust in order to further the goals of fieldwork. Ethnic members have not always been treated fairly by the larger society or understood in terms of their problems and needs. Some of them have already been exploited, studied without their consent, had their privacy invaded, and been harmed in some way. The least we can do is prevent these things from happening again. If we fail to use sound fieldwork ethics, then we not only dishonor the ethnic group we study, but we also dishonor research.

# Part II

The fieldwork experience, as described in chapter 4, incorporates different kinds of reasons for studying a group. These reasons may give some indication of how challenging it will be to interact with and collect data from a given population. Is it to know the group better so that one can deliver social services better? Is it to understand why certain populations hang out at a certain place in the community that may not seem all that desirable? Whatever the reason, establishing good rapport in order to have credibility with the group being studied becomes critical to data gathering.

Credibility and legitimacy are major aspects of building trust. As an experience for the fieldworker, taking good fieldnotes that can be compared over a time period and constantly reevaluated can help in identifying inconsistencies in information that reveal elements of distrust. Staying in the field long enough to gather these notes and being as objective as possible helps to maintain a clear perspective of the group and community.

To make the job of fieldwork easier, chapter 5 helps us see how ethnic communities can be organized and the type of cultural identity they may have. Though ethnic communities may seem homogeneous, there can be great diversity in the membership. This means that flexibility in interacting with ethnic members is important. From a research point of view, getting to know the community and the people's concerns is a top priority when doing fieldwork in ethnic communities. Sometimes this may require an accommodation of one's research topic to the interests and needs of the ethnic group being studied. Rather than seeing this as an unwelcome compromise, the researcher who goes into an ethnic community expecting to fully share his research topic, to incorporate the views of the community into his research, and to help the community benefit from his/her study will really be establishing a process in the community that others can trust.

Compare this with the way certain ethnic groups have been treated in the past where upward mobility was compromised because of the color of one's skin or where social services were more likely to result in stereotyping the users rather than neutrally assisting ethnic members. The background history of ethnic group relations makes it challenging to re-establish a basis for trust even when you are not the one who created the distrust in the first place.

*Chapter 4*

# The Fieldwork Experience

## THE ETHNOGRAPHIC TRADITION IN SOCIOLOGY

One of the richest forms of literature in sociology is the ethnography. This product of qualitative methodology using fieldwork techniques fires the imagination with powerful visions of social life among many different types of people and groups. Written in an easy narrative style, ethnographies provide insights into worlds seldom discussed by other researchers. They usually require years of observation and data collection to get the insider view that allows the reader to see what the group really is like. They also require much skill in interviewing and observing people in their natural environment in order to acquire the rich material that becomes carefully organized into an in-depth story of the subculture of a group. If an understanding of human behavior was what first attracted the author to sociology, the reading of ethnographies convinced her to stay in this field.

The ethnographic tradition in sociology began at the University of Chicago in the 1920s. Combining areas of social history, public concern, and sociological inquiry, the early ethnographies were sometimes encouraged by public agencies that wanted informative reports on certain subjects. An example of this is one of the author's favorite ethnographies, *The Hobo: The Sociology of the Homeless Man* by Nels Anderson. Published in 1923 by the University of Chicago Press, it was a study prepared for the Chicago Council of Social Agencies under the direction of the Committee on Homeless Men. Today, this subject would not be that relevant, but during the 1920s when there were thousands of migratory workers who were unemployed but looking for work, it was possible to see a lifestyle develop from the towns they created called "hobohemias." These towns were viewed with concern by social agencies because of the continuous ebb and flow into Chicago of homeless men. Nels Anderson was able to capture the beliefs and values, roles, and lifestyle of these homeless men we call hobos.

An equally absorbing ethnography is *The Taxi-Dance Hall: A Sociological Study in Commercialized Recreation and City Life.* Written in 1932 by Paul G. Cressey, the book was based on materials collected by the author when he was a caseworker and special investigator for the Juvenile Protective Association of Chicago. The taxi-dance halls were of concern to this association because they were considered questionable in character as a form of urban recreation. Since the taxi-dance halls offered the services of temporary companionship through dance in exchange for money, they were suspected of being linked to sex and vice.

In his ethnography, Cressey normalized the people and activities of the taxi-dance hall by taking an insider's view of the place. He could see the function such a form of recreation would serve in a city where many immigrant men passed through and where women were looking for work. These women were hired as dancers who worked for a dime a dance. As a classic in sociology, this fieldwork study using participant observation was able to show that there was a demand for the taxi-dance hall as a place for lonely, unattached men to socialize and for independent women to find jobs.

A later ethnography, *Tally's Corner,* by Elliot Liebow also focused on social problems in the inner city. Liebow chose to study African American street corner men in Washington D.C. during 1962 and 1963 using participant observation. Like the other two ethnographers, Liebow was trying to study a group of people that was difficult to reach by community agencies. He wanted to understand the lifestyle of low income Black males on their own terms so that new knowledge could be acquired that might improve services to families and children. Though he was a White male gathering data on Black males, Liebow managed to get enough of an insider's view that we can see the importance of the primary, face-to face relationships among the men of Tally's corner and the way they are able to enact their social and familial roles.

All three of the above ethnographies relate to ethnic groups in the United States and so they are relevant to our study of fieldwork. The ethnography of hobos by Nels Anderson was really a look at the plight of European male immigrants to the United States who formed a large group of unemployed men as the economy got worse, as well as those who suffer from job discrimination like African American and Mexican males. Many of them were single so they migrated from place to place looking for seasonal or part-time work. When the work ran out they would move on, usually riding the trains from state to state.

*The Taxi-Dance Hall* not only studied the American female who became a taxi-dance hall hostess in Chicago, but also her patrons that consisted of a large group of Asian males—mostly Filipino and some Chinese—and European male immigrants. Blacks were excluded from the social clubs because of racial segregation and Asians were excluded from everything else but the taxi-dance hall because of their color. The lack of Filipino women to date and marry was a factor in the Filipino males turning to the taxi-dance halls for socialization and companionship.

In *Tally's Corner*, we see a study of Black street corner men whose habits and personal lifestyles were unknown to the outside world until Elliot Liebow followed these men around and recorded their story. He raises the issue of his being White and wonders if that affected his ability to get accurate data from the Black street corner men. Though he felt it did not compromise his study, this is an issue that the author had raised earlier as being important for investigation. It is especially crucial when fieldwork is short-term or done as a one-shot experience. When fieldwork is done on a long-term basis, it is easier to see discrepancies in data as they get revealed over time, and one can make adjustments to the ethnographic narratives as the data are reassessed.

## ESTABLISHING TRUST AND CREDIBILITY

In reality the task for the fieldworker who studies a group different from his or her own can be fraught with all kinds of difficulties. Rosalie Wax has plenty of thoughts about this matter since she studied two different ethnic communities: Japanese Americans in American relocation centers during World War II and Native Americans on reservations. Her ideas about fieldwork in these communities are published in *Doing Fieldwork: Warnings and Advice*.

Rosalie Wax states that researchers who want to acquire an insider's view of a group would "tend to emphasize the importance of learning new forms of communication, new definitions of good behavior and evil behavior, new social roles, [and] new meanings for the phenomenon of everyday life" (Wax 1971, 4). However, she had to do much more than this as a newly recruited fieldworker in the Japanese relocation centers. She was the only non-Japanese researcher selected as part of a university-based interdisciplinary research project at the University of California–Berkeley. In the beginning, she was told to on no account give any data to the War Relocation Authority, which was looking for evidence that would incriminate any Japanese person as a spy. Under these conditions, her entrance into the field would hardly be ideal as far as establishing trust and credibility, since she could easily be mistaken for being a spy for the other side.

Wax mentions how distrustful the Japanese were of any Caucasian at the Tule Lake Internment site, and any Caucasian who entered their camp without a legitimate reason was believed to be a spy. This did not discourage her, and she immersed herself into the camp experience, getting involved with people of all ages and with different political leanings. After several months of fieldwork, Wax described her role and status as an "expert visitor" which translated into a visiting outsider who could understand what people were telling her (Ibid., 171). This is the type of role that evolves from continuous efforts to win the trust of people you study. However, in Wax's case we might wonder if she went overboard and got too involved with the people she studied. She ended up joining the Japanese in their political and quasi-military struggle against unfair policies toward the Japanese, which made her like an activist.

Boundary issues do concern the author since scientific neutrality and objectivity in interpreting data can be compromised. Yet, some fieldworkers will do almost anything to be accepted by the group they are studying, including joining in the community activities of that culture. Some of this is fine if it does not harm oneself physically and it fits one's status and role in the community. This was not the case with Wax's husband, who went with Wax to an Indian reservation. When he arrived there, the Indians defined him as a middle-age man of wealth and substance who was White. As such, he was not required to be skillful in any of the men's activities, and he was to be respected by the young men (Ibid., 272). However, he tried to demonstrate his manhood as a swimmer, and that wasn't required. He also tried to talk openly with the young men about their education, but they were quiet out of respect. In these cases, it is a lack of knowledge of cultural expectations that makes one overstep proper boundaries in interaction.

In both ethnic communities, Rosalie Wax was trying to gather accurate data about her research topics, and this required much patience and the hard work of finding out who would trust her. She realizes after her fieldwork experiences that most people will not believe what a stranger tells them, and they only learn to trust the stranger not by her research, but by the way she lives and acts and how she treats the people of the community (Ibid., 365). Wax also learned that Indians need lots of time to find out for themselves if they can trust White people. She and her husband were put to the test in the beginning by one family who tested their generosity and patience while the rest of the reservation community looked on. It wasn't until later, after she had passed the tests, that she was able to get a guide and interpreter. Similarly, at Tule Lake, Wax had to visit respondents for months and work hard on her Japanese lessons before they divulged important information. Trust requires the building of a friendly and communicative relationship, she says, that almost always involves a period of careful watching and judging on the part of community members (Ibid., 366).

Getting back to the idea of accuracy in collecting fieldwork data, Wax discusses the fieldworker as a fool at the end of her book. She states that it is inevitable to be made a fool of when you are visiting an ethnic group different from your own. You can get exploited, short-changed, even blackmailed, robbed, and fooled as community members mislead you and make fun of you (Ibid., 370). This is the stage when the fieldworker will wonder who she can trust and what materials were accurate that she collected. Being fooled would be most difficult to realize when a certain amount of naiveté on the part of the fieldworker makes her ethnocentric enough to believe that she will be welcome wherever she goes.

However, Wax states that being fooled has the advantage of increasing one's understanding (Ibid., 372). This is an important component in one's development as a fieldworker. Since trust is the key to establishing greater intimacy in a relationship and it does not come until much later in the fieldwork experience, a later assessment of data collected may be necessary for establishing accuracy.

## STRATEGIES FOR DOING FIELDWORK RESEARCH

There are several books available on how to do fieldwork, but the author finds two fieldwork books in particular to be useful for a beginning student. One is an old book with very basic ideas that can be easily applied. It is by Leonard Schatzman and Anselm Strauss, and it is called *Field Research: Strategies for a Natural Sociology.* A newer book is also very good, especially in getting at the experience of fieldwork. Bonnie Sunstein and Elizabeth Chiseri-Strater call it *FieldWorking: Reading and Writing Research.*

Whether one is approaching fieldwork from the disciplines of sociology or anthropology, the strategies are similar because the important thing is developing a new slant on life when studying a group of people different from one's own. It is like exploring a new world if you have the curiosity of a traveler or fine-tuning one's senses if you are alerting yourself to new experiences. Working in the field requires patience, but also a set of tools or guidelines, so the rest of this chapter will be spent on summarizing useful strategies. If the reader wants thorough discussions of fieldwork strategies, these can be found in the above textbooks. Keep in mind that fieldwork is preceded by a research goal that an individual develops, and it is this goal that forms the basis for doing fieldwork.

If we were to see fieldwork research as a progression of experiences, then we can start at the beginning, which is the point of entering the field. The author would call this the phase of educating one's self about the people, place, and events that are to be visited. Schatzman and Strauss say that one needs information about the principal people at the site, especially if it is an institution, and some history of the site with its succession of key persons, objectives, and beliefs (1973, 19). Sunstein and Chiseri-Strater emphasize the importance of understanding culture and subcultures before entering the field, which includes knowing the insider and outsider roles and being able to step outside the culture while also being involved with the people you study (Sunstein and Chiseri-Strater, 2002, 6–9). This implies being objective, but also understanding.

One of the best ways of stepping outside a culture is to try and do that with your own culture. In sociology, we have a field called ethnomethodology where the researcher studies the norms of his own culture. However, one cannot really understand how a norm works unless one sees it violated in public. Thus, the researcher will set up exercises where he may violate a norm, and by studying the reactions of people to his norm violation, will understand how the norm functions in its cultural setting. This is an interesting way of practicing objectivity.

Another way of practicing value neutrality that is more anthropological is to write about your culture as if it were the most foreign culture in the world or universe. Your descriptions should sound like Horace Miner's study of the Nacirema, a most delightful perception of a group's cultural behaviors and beliefs (Miner 1956). By expecting differences or strangeness, the fieldworker may be delighted to experience sameness. This is easier to handle than the other way around.

After the education phase of fieldwork, negotiating one's way into the group or setting is important, and this may be as simple as getting permission from someone in a leadership position, or it may be as difficult as finding the right informant who will be a guide in helping you get to know other people in the community. The assumption here is that one cannot just go charging up to a group of people and say you want to study them. You need to follow proper procedures that will maximize your ability to get accurate information from people.

Once you have permission to enter a community or other setting, you may want to figure out how you will proceed with your fieldwork. Schatzman and Strauss call this getting organized, and it would include a mapping operation which is a neighborhood tour to check out people, things and activities, a sampling selection of specific sites and people to observe, a time frame in which to do the work, a selection of the actual research location, and acquiring resources and a more sharpened focus of interest (Schatzman and Strauss 1973). Sunstein and Chiseri-Strater recommend a research portfolio at this stage of fieldwork that includes working files for tracking learning and documenting work throughout the research process (Sunstein and Chiseri-Strater 2002, 43). To do this portfolio, the fieldworker needs to know how to take field notes because this is a vital part of gathering information.

Field notes can be as precise as tape recording entire conversations from people and transcribing them exactly word for word. However, this is very tedious and can take forever to do. Another way of doing field notes is to make them a construction of your own field experience (Ibid., 56). It means that they will represent your perspective of things based on what you saw and heard. They are not intended to be something that can be duplicated by others. Since one cannot always use a tape recorder when out in the field, your notes may be highlighting only the most important things you experience. These notes will then be developed into a more comprehensive picture of what is going on at the site or with the people you study.

After these beginning phases of fieldwork, the experience of doing field-work is one of looking for details, understanding cultural meanings, looking for new leads, and getting involved with the people you study. Schatzman and Strauss emphasize the strategies for watching, listening, recording, and analyzing in their book. They see the researcher as someone who "generally accepts whatever he sees and hears at face value; he denigrates no motives. He does not visibly take sides on arguments among members no matter how much he may be invited to do so" (Schatzman and Strauss 1973). Further-more, "the researcher must be a good role-taker; that is, he must 'stand' with each respondent in the latter's relationship to the universe, and view it and its associated vocabulary from that perspective" (Ibid., 69).

However, one does not need to be this formal when doing fieldwork. A person can also listen in a neighborly way, just like one would if listening to a group of people one knows. This type of listening may help you begin to see how conversations are really stories that people are telling. Stories about life can give you family history as well as perceptions of people's real world. In the marriage and family therapy area, a psychotherapy called Narrative Therapy, developed by Michael White and David Epston, encourages clients to talk about how they see things when they have a problem (White and Epston 1990). The stories they tell reflect how they are coping with their problem and how it frustrates them and keeps them from functioning. As they begin to look at their problem as something outside of themselves, they are able to see that they are not the problem, but instead a target for the problem. This allows them to find ways to outsmart the problem. As they start to outsmart the problem, changes occur in their life and they are able to tell a more renewing and powerful story about themselves, which is really a way to overcome the problem.

Such is the power of a story, and when it is coming from many different people, it should produce enough data to help one piece together the culture of a group. This is when the field notes get organized into a text that demonstrates the fieldworker's skill at writing for an audience. Writing strategies can include being experiential (firsthand accounts of your experiences), rhetorical (referring to your voice, purpose, and audience), and aesthetic (the use of artistic ways to represent what you studied; Sunstein and Chiseri-Strater 2002, 448–9). The telling of your story based on the data you collected about a group of people is the final phase of doing fieldwork. It is the final product of all your efforts as a researcher, and it gives your observations and perceptions coherency. It includes linking ideas, raising questions about your experience, and analyzing what you found. Analyzing requires the working of one's thought processes to get meaning out of the data. It is like questioning the data to see what it will communicate. If the researcher "has developed no exciting ideas, he must tease them out of the data, and when he gets them feed them back for a test—that is, search for supporting and negative evidence" (Schatzman and Strauss 1973, 120).

After the field notes are written in text form, revisions can occur several times so that the message becomes more clear and focused. The fieldworker may get new ideas along the way and find that learning is occurring in surprising ways. That is the nice thing about writing up one's field notes into a story; one learns to see the people and culture from a new angle and to notice things that were hidden earlier. Usually, anthropologists and sociologists make comments about their learning experience after writing their stories because they get many new insights after they write.

Though the actual process of doing fieldwork from beginning to end may not be this simple and compact, it is definitely rewarding and usually very enjoyable. It can be an arduous undertaking that requires months of actual experience before the fieldworker gets comfortable with the population he or she studies, but at the same time it brings out one's social and interactional skills in marvelous ways.

# Chapter 5

# Ethnic Groups and Communities

When dealing with ethnic populations in urban areas, one of the most important things to keep in mind is that it is virtually impossible to say that all members of an ethnic community are alike. Likewise, communities vary a great deal from each other depending on the social characteristics of their members so that they could be different based on such things as age, religion, or class, or each community could have a diversity of lifestyles and values. For example, African American communities will show subcultural variations depending on whether they are in the South or outside that region, or whether they are urban or rural (Pinkney, 1969, 69). With Mexican Americans, important factors in their diversity can be the result of immigration patterns or area of settlement (Moore 1970, 55). For Japanese Americans, generation may be a very significant characteristic, important enough to warrant the separate designations of Issei, Nisei, and Sansei to create categories of people that are distinct both culturally and socially.

## THE NATURE OF COMMUNITIES[1]

The urban community is very different from the small town, rural community that the anthropologist ordinarily studies as a participant observer. A common body of theory which dates from the late-19th century (Durkheim 1933; Redfield 1947; Tonnies 1957) suggests that urban areas are to a greater or lesser extent disorganized, as compared to "folk" communities, which are assumed to be "simple" in structure or noncomplex, organized, and homogeneous. Furthermore, as migrants moved into urban areas, they were commonly assumed to suffer disorganization and even personality disintegration, resulting in such things as rises in crime rates.

Yet, cross-cultural studies, done in such diverse places as colonial Africa and among American Indians in the urban centers of the United States, suggest that these long-standing assumptions are untrue (Eames and Schwab 1964; Waddell and Watson 1971; Abu-Laghod 1961). Rather than disorganization, urban areas have a multiplex and shifting organization made up of "dynamic" communities and subcultures. A dynamic community consists of a set of centers for social interaction and information exchange. Thus, a given ethnic population could be broken up into many communities, some of which may be at odds with each other. Furthermore, the communities could be scattered the length of an urban area, with no sign of their identity visible to the outsider, or be contained within a single neighborhood.

These ideas, of course, have implications for community social interaction, so it is important to look more deeply at the nature of communities. In order to understand how ethnic communities function, it is necessary to identify some of the processes at work that create a community environment. These include such things as boundary maintenance, social identity formation, and acculturation.

## Boundary Maintenance

Although there may not be even any large degree of voluntary segregation, the people will generally maintain themselves apart from others through a sense of pride and loyalty. They will do this by using such devices as language, dress, and membership in community organizations.

## Social Identity Formation

The mechanisms by which social boundaries are maintained can become important factors in social identity for the individual as well as the group. They enable the culture of a group to be maintained within a demarcated setting and allow for the acknowledgement of individual and group heritage. The degree to which a person is mapped into the community and his/her social importance may depend to a large extent on the proper use of such identity-boundary cues.

## Acculturation

This is defined as changes in lifestyle due to prolonged contact with and acceptance of traits from another ethnic population. A migrant population will indeed accept new ideas and habits from the host culture; however, it should be borne in mind that (a) there are degrees of this, and (b) a distinction between acculturation and accommodation should be made. We might expect to find vast differences among individuals from the migrant population, ranging from those who refuse to make any change to accommodate to life in the host culture, to those who wish nothing more than to be absorbed into its mainstream. In between, of course, will be those who make such accommodations as they feel are inevitable or somehow desirable, and retain as much of their ancestral culture as possible. The key to understanding this phenomenon is psychological identification—the forming of an emotional predilection toward a new role model of either the host culture or those who have made a successful compromise with it. Changes in behavior due to some compromise with the new life might not be permanent if the people returned to their pre-migration ethnic culture. However, changes made in attitudes, values, and behaviors due to identification with a new role model might well be permanent and constitute acculturation.

Any attempt to study migrant or subcultural ethnic people should attempt to measure this degree of change and acculturation, or at least be aware that it exists with those individuals one uses as informants or as respondents in a study. The following is a list of things one should find out about the ethnic population: (a) are the people making changes which they consider desirable "back home," but could not permit? (b) are they evolving a lifestyle which is a compromise between the new and the ethnic? (c) are they making the best of a bad bargain and accommodating as smoothly as they can? (d) are they becoming acculturated and heading toward absorption in the main stream of modern life?

Knowing such things as the nature of the community organization, the number and variety of subcultures within a community or urban area, and the cultural enclaves within communities where traditional customs and ways persist will be useful in giving the fieldworker a sense of direction in his/her research and community orientation. Within the enclaves, one finds persons from the ethnic origin area tending to live where they are able to satisfy their emotional needs by the creation of interaction and information exchange centers. This enables them to remain isolated from contact with the larger society or to avoid or limit their contacts with members of the host group. The implications of this are that they would tend to perpetuate the life way, values, and worldviews of their subculture, to limit their contact with larger societal agencies and their policies, and to have distinct histories and methods of adaptation to American society that must be understood by the fieldworker in order to deal with the people.

## CHARACTERISTICS OF COMMUNITY GROUPS

Because of the nature of ethnic communities, research on ethnic groups will produce a variety of responses even when respondents are members from roughly the same geographical location. Some of the sociological variables that will affect ethnic members' responses to interview questions, include socioeconomic status or class background, generation, region of settlement, and size of the ethnic community. Some, or all, of these factors will affect the degree of assimilation of ethnic members to American ways, so that even within a given community it will be possible to find members who know quite a lot about the ethnic culture and others who have lost an understanding of many customs and practices. Actually, there may not be a clear geographical sense of an ethnic community anymore, and individuals may belong to many community groups depending on their interests and identifications. Even the Samoan community cannot be clearly demarcated on a map, though there exists Samoan social institutions and organizations (Shu and Satele 1977, 8).

On the other hand, there are certain characteristics that bind the people together such as language in the case of Mexican Americans (Gomez 1972, 7) or the experience of intensive and continuous discrimination as among African Americans, which has forced them into a position of a self-conscious minority (Pinkney 1969, 170). American ethnic minorities have historically gone through periods of residential segregation, which has resulted in their isolation from the dominant society and the retention of their cultural beliefs and practices.

Research on community groups can be influenced by these ways in which ethnic members regard themselves and how they feel others outside their community view them, especially in their status as immigrants or ethnic minorities. Like the Asian people, other ethnic groups are very sensitive about the image they project to both their own members and others outside their community, and this concept of "face" will determine how pleased or displeased they will be with research topics and results.

Among the people of the Pacific Islands and many Native American groups, this concern with maintaining "face" results in individuals being unwilling to risk looking bad in the eyes of others or appearing negative through research findings. This makes it difficult for individual community members to assist the researcher or fieldworker in gathering data for a study, because the community people may not be willing to disclose pertinent information even to them. However, these informants or consultants may still cooperate with the researcher even though they know the research can endanger the image of the ethnic community, and this places them in a potentially awkward situation.

The cooperating community member may also face the problem of role conflict. This situation can occur when the person is caught between two groups who view him and his situation with differing beliefs and expectations, or he has two opposing roles that lead to conflicting conceptions of his duties and behaviors. Because these difficulties may arise, it is important that one acquire the cooperation of those who can most favorably influence the members of the ethnic community. These persons should help to ease some of the community apprehension before the research is begun and help to monitor the project as it is being developed. However, the fieldworker should be aware of the extent of this community feeling about "saving face." Even with variations in cultural retention and social characteristics existing among community members, there may always be certain sentiments shared in common by these members that keep the researcher in the role of "outsider."

## ACHIEVING ACCESS TO ETHNIC
## MINORITY COMMUNITIES

Research in ethnic communities began developing a grassroots consciousness after the ethnic movements of the 1970s. Professionals were now starting to realize that maximum community collaboration was essential to obtaining accurate research results. It was during this time in 1980 that the author attended a workshop on Asian Pacific research held in San Francisco. Several important points were raised on methodology by the community members, agency personnel, and academicians who attended this workshop. These points included establishing a role in the community, asking the right questions, having some payoff for the community, getting constituency involvement in the research, and considering the community in research plans.

Establishing a role in the community was mentioned for the purpose of getting firsthand knowledge on a research topic from the point of view of the ethnic group itself. To do this, the researcher would have to put aside his research hat for awhile and be nonscientific as he/she mingles in the community like "one of the people." This would put the researcher in a humanistic role where an interest in the people of the community and their concerns become primary.

Asking the right questions has to do with knowing what is relevant to community members and what is appropriate to ask. To many ethnic members, questions on age, socioeconomic status, occupation, and education may not be relevant. For the researcher they are important because they help him to group people's responses into certain categories that are social scientifically useful. Yet, the right questions for the people may have more to do with how they can do something or why things are the way they are, rather than what their social characteristics are. Thus, they would not be concerned with research topics that are purely academic, such as their level of achievement compared to another ethnic group or their degree of assimilation to American life. They have specific problems that concern them, and they would like the researcher to find answers to them in order to bring about changes in their lives.

Some ethnic members will not know how to answer a quantitative question such as family size, because they are used to thinking in terms of the qualitative dimensions of largeness and smallness. Or, they may not be able to answer a question as a single individual because they are used to thinking of themselves as a member of a family group, and it is the answer coming from parents and other group members that is decisive. One finds this to be the case with many Asian people and with Mexican Americans when it comes to health care (Clark 1959). On other questions that deal with sensitive areas, such as income and occupation, many ethnic members may have a tendency to under-report or over-report the information mainly because of modesty or not wanting to appear in a lesser income category or occupation than others. Because of variations such as these in perception and behavior, researchers should be careful about the questions they ask respondents, being mindful of sensitive topics and the level of difficulty in answering questions that are not familiar to people.

The payoff to the community is an ethical concern of researchers in how to give respondents and research participants some reward for their contribution to the study. Many times this matter is not considered carefully because researchers are in a hurry to finish their work and leave the community as soon as possible. However, the payoff to the community is essential and can take a number of forms. It can include paying individuals money for their participation, giving gifts of some type, helping to make changes within the community that will benefit the people, sending research results back to community agencies so they can provide better services for their clients, and training community members in research skills so that they can stay in the neighborhood and continue to research problems of concern to the people. Lastly, one can simply inform the people of research results which, minimally, researchers should do anyway.

Any topic of research will affect a certain group of people, so it is important that there be constituency involvement in research. Since these people have a stake in the outcome of research, they would be interested in knowing the results of research. As ethnic members, they will have a "special" insight into community problems that may be very different from that of the researcher, so their "concept of reality" should be included in the research process. Their involvement in the research as trained assistants or consultants is invaluable for a proper definition of an ethnic problem and interpretation of data.

When ethnic members are not involved in research, community members may complain that they were victims of research. They will find that things were said about them that do not coincide with their view of reality. If the results of research are negative and make community members look bad in the eyes of the public, this can be disturbing as well as disgraceful to people who pride themselves on their ethnic heritage. After such an experience, it is not surprising that community members would distrust researchers and be less willing to cooperate with them at another time.

By having ethnic members participate in research, the gap between the community and academia is lessened and both groups are able to benefit from each other's insights and expertise. For example, it is not easy for community members to develop skills in proposal writing so that they themselves can acquire funds for research, but the skills of the academic person can be used to assist community members to write these proposals. Community members, in turn, can help the researcher develop further insights into the research topic and goals.

It is for this reason that researchers should show a consideration for the community in their research plans. Ethnic members do have concerns about various aspects of research, and the fieldworker should adapt himself to these concerns as much as possible, even tailoring the research project to the needs of the ethnic population. In order to do this, it is necessary that he ascertain the nature of the community, determining which segment of the group he is dealing with and why, and know the exact nature of the data to be collected. He can then discuss his research with the ethnic members to make sure he is asking the right questions. If the fieldworker ends up with problems or questions that are not relevant to community members, he can rebuild his set of questions along the way as research proceeds. In this way, he is more likely to receive cooperation from the people because the questions are brought into line with their expectations. Listening to the suggestions of community members, who are asked to assist or participate in the research, can make a big difference in the success of the research project.

Too often, failure of a research project or program is attributed to the respondents rather than to faulty innovative techniques. However, the researcher should keep in mind that others may not use the same criteria in judging research competence and excellence as he does. He may feel that his credentials give him credibility and authority in the community of research, but the ethnic people may consider him a "complete jerk" for what he is doing. The characteristics which can influence the success of a research project include such things as the researcher's personality and communication skills, his affiliations with others (in actuality and in the minds of the people), his technical competence, and his approach to the people as a researcher (the personal, formal, and demonstrative manner in which he presents the research to the people). Naturally, successful communication with the people is determined by these things, which affects the impression they have of the researcher.

The cooperation of ethnic members is also determined by the advantages they feel they will derive through their participation in the research. This must be coupled with how much labor and time they must put into the project and how active or passive they must be as participants. Motivation, though, can be solicited by the fieldworker once it is ascertained by him and demonstrated by community members. Thus, individuals might participate in research if economic (new supplies or resources in the community), medical, or educational benefits were to be received.

The researcher should also be aware of how to identify and possibly utilize local culture that includes traditional leadership, language, foods, and customs. He should be aware that there may be many forms of leadership in a community depending on which segment he is dealing with, and these forms of leadership could be in such areas as administration, education, religion, and public opinion in informal and formal organizations. Leadership ties in with the social structure, and there can be many forms of social organization depending on whether one is speaking of a traditional, ethnic, or modern community. These forms of social organization include kinship groups, classes, castes, and segments of society recognized by tradition or political and religious authority. Thus, there can be several parallel hierarchies within the community with different purposes and viewpoints.

In conclusion, the data from this workshop is consistent with the conclusions formed by others doing ethnic community research in order to improve social service delivery systems. The staff of the Asian American Community Mental Health Training Center of Los Angeles has strongly supported the idea of direct involvement of Asian American/Pacific Islanders in the entire research process. This involvement should take place in the generation of the research topic, the development of the methodology, the conducting of the research, and the dissemination and implementation of research results (Chikahisa et al. 1976). By using this procedure, one avoids the risk of producing erroneous "scientific" conclusions that do not reflect the view of the community people. Even when survey research is done in ethnic communities, it can also follow this same principle. For example, one research study on Japanese Americans did make use of the viewpoint of the people. This was a survey of the group's view of mental health concepts, which was conducted to find out why this population was under-using mental health services and to find ways to develop services more responsive to the people (Okano 1977). These approaches to ethnic community research are a much needed step toward making the voice of the ethnic community heard to professionals and toward developing research that is useful to both academic and community people.

The limited data from the Pilot Ethnic Research Training Project conducted earlier by the author will also be used to examine potential problems in doing research in ethnic communities. Before that is done, though, it is helpful to understand some things about group behavior and interaction between ethnic groups in American society. Since problem areas vary with each ethnic group, it is important to examine aspects of history and culture that might make a difference in understanding the existence of these problems. For example, research in African American communities may suffer from low response rates, high attrition rates, community protests of the research effort and ethnic group questioning of the validity and accuracy of the data collected. Yet these problems, which relate to other ethnic groups as well, may not have much meaning unless they are examined within the backdrop of this group's experience with racism and discrimination over the generations and the members' subsequent distrust of researchers (Turner et al. 2004, 263).

What is important to consider in understanding ethnic groups in the United States is the issue of trust. Though this is an area that is more often the focus of psychologists and counselors, theoretically it can be very useful in explaining the behaviors and attitudes of ethnic members toward outsiders, whether they are of a different race, ethnicity, religion, or class. Our long history of being a nation in which majority/minority group relations exists and dominates the landscape of democracy points out the lack of trust between people as they eye each other with conflict and lack of acceptance. Prejudice and discrimination have been breeding under these conditions for decades. If trust, according to Webster's dictionary, is a faith or confident belief in the integrity, ability, or character of a person, then distrust would be an inability to rely on a person's integrity, ability, or character for any reason. Going further with this definition, one can say that trust is something that must be built up, and it is created through the experiences that people have with others. When relationships are positive, one is more likely to see trust being formed. When relationships are negative, distrust can occur.

Each ethnic group to the United States has had a set of experiences that determine its chances for upward mobility and acceptance by the host society. One can hypothesize that the more negative the historical and relational experiences have been for an ethnic group with the host society, the more distrust would be built up by that group over time. This distrust can come from the host society as well. Normally, we study the host society or majority group and see this group's negativity in terms of racism, discrimination, and prejudice toward minority group members, but there is clearly distrust there as well. When the minority group member harbors negative feelings toward the host society in the way of distrust, this distrust should result in different ways that minority group members perceive outsiders and also how they behave toward them.

Groups that have experienced more negative treatment by the host society historically should exhibit more distrust of researchers than those groups who have had less negative treatment. This is one of the hypotheses that will be used in the following chapters to explain the different responses given by ethnic group members when interviewed about researchers. This does not mean that cultural differences are unimportant. In itself, a cultural difference could determine whether relationships will be positive or negative due to the misunderstandings people have about each other.

However, cultural differences seem to diminish over time much easier than negative majority/minority group conflicts. Assimilation is a strong force in this country that does make a group more Western over time. However, it is a neutral process. Negative experiences that lead to distrust can continue into each generation and show up in ways that have little to do with material culture. An interesting example of this can be found in Harlow and Dundes' study of White and African American responses to the September 11, 2001 attack of New York's Twin Towers by hijacked airplanes. While the nation as a whole demonstrated grief and outward patriotism during this time, African American and White student focus group respondents reacted very differently from each other. The African American students were more likely than the White students to not feel as connected to American society in a way where they could patriotically say that was "our Trade Center that was destroyed." Nor were they feeling closer to other Americans during this time or were as shocked by the events as the White students (2004). This lack of identification with a "core" American society would indicate an estrangement from the majority group based on distrust.

Another example of African American distrust can be seen in the under-utilization of community services. If an agency is not staffed by African Americans, it may not be used by several members of this group because of a fear of discrimination or poor treatment by the staff. Even when proper fieldwork etiquette is being used, African Americans may still not trust an outside agency. Henderson found that when a particular church was selected to deliver an Alzheimer caregiver's service, nobody showed up. It was assumed that a church would be a good place to have the meeting because so many African Americans go to church. However, he found out that people were loyal to their own church and would not go to a free service in their community if it was at somebody else's church. A more neutral place would have been a library, to gradually build up the trust of the people until they got used to the service (2005).

By focusing on several ethnic groups, those targeted by the Pilot Ethnic Research Training Project, and examining who they are as a people socially, historically, and psychologically, it will be possible to understand how they might react to researchers and to being respondents in research studies. Keep in mind that when ethnic members are interviewed for research purposes, it is extremely important that the researcher know a few things about the people and their community, as well as their history and relations with the host society. Without this knowledge, research may not be successful or have the cooperation of the people.

Most ethnic groups are very sensitive about outsiders coming into their community to study them, especially if they are groups that have been mistreated in the past, are new to this country, have had some negative experiences in adjusting here, or are people who have been studied in the past but were not presented with the research idea or its results. One can also hypothesize that, today, people living in urban areas may be more distrustful of anyone trying to solicit information from them because of the rash of door-to-door crimes and identity thefts going on. Therefore, the researcher should not only be aware of the proper courtesies to extend toward ethnic groups that go beyond knowledge of his own Western culture, but to also offer signs of credibility that he is a researcher affiliated with a legitimate organization or institution.

Though the emphasis in the book takes a somewhat negative approach to relationships, it does not presume that all relationships between researchers and ethnic members are negative. In fact, successful research is the hallmark of positive encounters between people or an eventual understanding between them, and we have plenty of classic studies that demonstrate this. Nor is this book trying to reinforce the negative literature that was previously done about ethnic groups in earlier decades. Many of the ethnic groups studied in this book may still suffer from lower socioeconomic status, but this book is looking at the viable side of ethnic communities even though members can point out problems within their communities. Lastly, this book is not presuming that ethnic minorities always stand apart from whites and see them as the "oppressor." On a day-to-day basis, one would not even notice any sources of tension or discomfort between the majority and minority groups, except in certain situations. However, it would be disturbing to pretend that these tensions do not exist. While some of the negative encounters between ethnic groups and the majority group will be described in the following chapters, one should keep in mind that many more positive experiences do take place between individuals that lead to, if not a positive relationship, at least an accommodation.

A final note about studying ethnic groups can be made in terms of their in-group diversity. As mentioned at the beginning of the chapter, we cannot say that all members of an ethnic community are alike. One can go further to say that members of the same ethnic group can form different communities based on socioeconomic class, for example, or region of the country. While one would expect variations in responses to researchers based on demographic variables such as class, gender, age, political affiliation, and others, it is possible and even likely that ethnic groups who share a common history and cultural heritage can still feel a sense of ingroup-outgroup affiliation based on the color of their skin and the perception of others toward them. Some individuals may have had little or no experiences of prejudice or discrimination based on their life experiences, but most are aware of these things happening to others. This would imply that not all members of an ethnic group are equally victimized or oppressed, but the problem still remains.

In the rest of this book, the chapters will focus on the cultural diversity of populations living in the United States, but with a particular look at those situated in Southern California. In order to find out more about the culture of certain ethnic groups and their attitudes toward university researchers doing fieldwork in their community, the author conducted a small study in the summer of 1980 on the following ethnic groups: African Americans, Japanese Americans, specific Southeast Asian groups, Mexican Americans, and Samoans. Members from these communities were intensely interviewed on a number of questions by interviewers who were members of their own ethnic group. The data collected by these interviewers produced a number of insights on these ethnic groups and their culture that would be useful to fieldworkers, researchers, community workers, and anyone providing services to ethnic communities. The information acquired from this study is intended to make students and faculty aware of how ethnic members can feel about being the object of research. It also takes into consideration the way ethnic people would like to see research being conducted in their community. By knowing the social and cultural expectations that ethnic members have for outsiders, it is hoped that fewer transgressions into areas that are offensive to these people will be made. It is also the hope of the author that this research data will add to a greater understanding of these ethnic groups and also improve people's daily interaction with culturally diverse groups in general.

The results of the research are presented in the remaining portion of this book, with each ethnic community being treated separately. Several comments need to be made about the chapters as they focus on specific ethnic groups. All of the chapters, except for the ones on African Americans and the Vietnamese, will begin with a wider coverage of the family of ethnic groups that the group belongs to. For example, chapter 8 will cover Asian Americans more generally and then focus on Japanese Americans. Chapter 9 will describe Latino populations and then go into Mexican Americans. And chapter 10 will cover Pacific Islanders first and then focus on the Samoans. This coverage will allow the reader to see how similar types of ethnic groups may encounter the same problems that the group focused on is encountering.

However, this coverage of the specific ethnic groups is inadequate to really understand their history and group relations with the dominant society. It is important that other textbooks on race and ethnic relations be studied to get a deeper coverage of these issues. The materials in this book were presented, selectively, to highlight issues of trust and distrust, so they should not be taken out of this context. Unfortunately, the groups selected are not inclusive of all the ethnic groups that are relevant to study in terms of trust issues. A big omission is a chapter on Native Americans. This group was not included because the author did not have interview/survey data on this population. Other ethnic groups such as Puerto Ricans, Cubans, and eastern Europeans are relevant for their East Coast settlement, but could not be included in this study. However, other textbooks covering these groups may reveal similar experiences in ethnic relations to those covered here. The reader is cautioned to note the sample size of respondents in this study when evaluating and interpreting their statements. The comments of respondents reflect their own personal opinions and, therefore, cannot be generalized to all members of the ethnic group, especially when such great diversity exists among them.

## NOTE

1. The author is indebted to Dr. Ken Kuykendall for his assistance in developing this section. Prior to his retirement, Dr. Kuykendall was professor of anthropology at Calif. State Univ.–Dominguez Hills.

*Part III*

The Vietnamese and other Southeast Asians came to the United States in large numbers after the fall of Vietnam. How they experienced this country depended on their nation's earlier history and the reason for their immigration to the United States. The Vietnamese adapted more quickly and easily to American society than the Lao Hmong, who were disadvantaged by their mountain-farming background and lack of contact with urban, western environments. However, both groups managed to maintain many aspects of traditional culture today, despite living in the United States for several decades.

Their issues of trust relate to both how they saw Americans, even before coming here, and how they were treated as an ethnic group once they came here. While they value American society for its educational opportunities, they were less likely to give up their strong family-centered values upheld by Confucianist/Buddhist traditions. Their trust in the researcher or fieldworker could be based on how respectful he/she is of Asian formalities, especially before conducting research. This is where understanding nonverbal communication becomes important.

African Americans value education too, but they have had a long, bitter history of being denied the same rights as others. Their issue of trust relates to treatment, whether it is one-on-one treatment in the workplace, how they get served in restaurants and at public agencies, or how the researcher perceives them as subjects to be studied. Trust may be related to subtle things like being listened to and being understood, or having one's opinion accepted and acknowledged. Indifference, lack of acknowledgment, and being distant and elitist are all indications that one is not important or valued, and this could be perceived as leading to treatment that is unfair, harmful, and rude.

The conditions for encouraging trust building would be making positive connections with members of the community through identifying group concerns, through the active participation of ethnic members in all stages of the research, and through remaining in touch with community members to implement beneficial research findings. African Americans know their community and its networks. It is time the fieldworker and researcher knew it too and utilized it appropriately.

Japanese Americans today may have less distrust of the dominant society than other ethnic groups. Their day-to-day treatment is not fraught with the type of social injury or psychological distress that African Americans may experience. However, their in-group trust, as shaped by culture and historical events, is so intact that it may inadvertently lead to distrust of other groups. Sporadic experiences of prejudice and discrimination based on skin color and Asian features could reinforce the distrust, and earlier memories of Japanese incarceration during World War II and lack of equal opportunities in its aftermath could enhance this distrust.

This distrust shows up to some extent in the research data presented on Japanese Americans. For example, they may not trust a researcher whose study does not benefit the community. Their community concerns may focus on things like spousal abuse, ethnic identification, counseling receptivity, inter-ethnic marriages, elderly care giving, and drug abuse. If the researcher is not interested in these areas, they may feel their participation is a waste of time. Yet, on the other hand, some Japanese who are more traditional may be reluctant to reveal anything negative in their family because they will lose face. The researcher would need to be careful in handling sensitive questions with the older generation and those more traditional. Other things that would need to be negotiated to build trust would be treating Japanese Americans as equals rather than as a minority group and being aware of each person's generational identity. Cultural differences are not an issue since the Japanese have been in the United States for a long time, but they would be sensitive to being treated as subjects as when they were in relocation centers.

Mexican Americans are a diverse group based on generation, immigration history, socioeconomic status, and acculturation. Because of lack of knowledge of this diversity, it is easy for the larger society to misperceive Mexican Americans as recent immigrants or "illegal" immigrants. These misperceptions can lead to stereotypes and discrimination that is the basis for Mexican distrust of the majority group. With a long history in the United States of being seen as "working class," despite upward mobility and middle class status for many Mexican Americans, a strong family culture and extended family network provides insularity from the larger society. This insularity, which is also protective, can make inner-group trust strong at the same time that it reinforces distrust of the larger society. Mexican Americans value family harmony and like to offer guests a person-oriented hospitality. This cultural trait is also expected from others, that is, to be treated in a personal way. When this does not happen, it is easy to see how distrust can occur.

The last chapter in this section is on Samoan Americans, an ethnic group whose culture and history is very different from the other groups that were presented. Their inclusion in this book is important in order to see how trust can be related to cultural understanding. Distrust is then related to negative or offensive behaviors shown by outsiders when they do not properly observe cultural norms, expectations, proper behavior, and respective ways. When an ethnic group's culture is so different from American culture, it is not difficult to see how misunderstandings and conflicts can occur between people.

Evidence of this lack of trust is seen in Samoan Americans' reaction to Margaret Mead's early book on Samoa. Because her research discussed the sexual behavior of Samoans, which is a tabooed subject, they felt she portrayed their community in an offensive way. It has been a long time since Mead's study was done, and Samoan Americans do value education and research that helps their community, but they are still sensitive to how cultural violations can hurt their image. Thus, it is understandable for them to distrust a researcher who knows very little about them or their ways.

# Chapter 6

# The Vietnamese and Other Southeast Asians

## THE VIETNAMESE

Arriving in the United States since 1975, when the Vietnam War ended, Vietnamese refugees were the most visible Southeast Asian group in the United States and the group most known to the American people. Their large presence in Southern California, especially in a community called "Little Saigon" in Orange County, California, has made them a good group to study.

As an ethnic group adapting to American society, the Vietnamese represent different levels and types of assimilation. Their original culture was heavily influenced by Chinese Confucianism and their language is comprised of three main dialects—Hanoi, Saigon, and Hue dialects (Thinh 1979, 2–3). These three dialects correspond to the North, South, and Central areas of Vietnam.

The Vietnamese Chinese formed a sizeable group of refugees from Victnam. They were sometimes referred to as the "ethnic Chinese" or the "Boat People." As a minority group within their nation of Vietnam, the Chinese were always business-oriented, owning and operating many of the large and small merchandise, food, and service establishments that would cater to all groups and classes of Vietnamese people (Hang 1980, 18). They spoke both Chinese and Vietnamese and have contributed in a major way to the economy of their country through business (Thinh 1979, 3). As part of the second wave of Vietnamese refugees to the United States, post-1975, their experience has been one of hardship and trauma as they left Vietnam on boat journeys to asylum countries, with sometimes long stays in refugee camps before settlement in the United States. The first wave of refugees came in 1975 just before the fall of Saigon to Communist rule. These 130,000 upper class and highly educated elite Vietnamese were flown out of the country as

65

part of an evacuation effort to assist these individuals who were affiliated with the United States government or held high level military positions (Kibria 2002, 181–83).

Since the turn of the century, Vietnam has been under French Colonial rule, under Japanese occupation during World War II, and under the influence of Americans during the Vietnam War. These intense interactions with foreign powers may have helped the Vietnamese people adapt to other cultures, but they would also bring out conflicts in relationships. The struggle to gain independence from the French Colonial government would create some animosity toward the French, but it would also pitch Vietnamese families against each other because of different political ideologies (Leung and Boehnlein 1996, 299). This situation would get much more pronounced in 1954 when the Geneva Agreement created two Vietnams with different political ideologies: one under communism in the North and the other with a more democratic government in the South.

The Vietnam War exacerbated the situation as the two Vietnams fought each other. The families from the North trying to escape communism fled to the South, but the South became no sanctuary when the Saigon Government collapsed in 1975. This is when large numbers of Vietnamese left the country, many times without intact families. Wars create trauma, alienation, and losses among family members. Coming to a foreign country, sometimes through many different avenues, creates extreme hardships that make adaptation to a host society difficult. This is probably why "Little Saigon" was so attractive and became such a large Vietnamese community, complete with rival political ideologies, but still a home away from home to many immigrants from Vietnam.

Today, many Vietnamese travel routinely from Southern California back to their homeland. The author visited Vietnam from December 26, 2002 to January 9, 2003, to see how this communist nation had evolved since the Vietnam War. Tourism is encouraged by the country now, so one will see Japanese tourists in large numbers, as well as visitors from the United States and other countries. Is there a strong Vietnamese culture in Vietnam? Absolutely, and despite the cultural influences left behind by France, Japan, and the United States, the Vietnamese dialects predominate and communist isolation has encouraged them. Though some Vietnamese in Vietnam speak French or English quite fluently, many others speak only Vietnamese. The most visible French legacy in Vietnam would be the French bread and pastries, while the Japanese legacy might be seen in large hotels. The effects of the presence in Vietnam of Americans can be seen in war equipment left by soldiers, in museums showing the bombings of Vietnamese towns by Americans and their torturing of Vietnamese villagers, and in the booby traps set for American soldiers shown to tourists as they visit places like the Cu

Chi Tunnels north of Saigon. The American image is inconsistent as vendors welcome the tourist money that Americans bring in to the countryside, but yet remind them of how much destruction they caused to the countryside and the people during the Vietnam War. Village vendors lure tourists to their stalls, some with an English perfected during the Vietnam War, while the Communist government encourages tourists to buy goods from disabled children who were the products of napalm bombs dropped on their villages.

These inconsistencies could really be the way the Vietnamese are loyal to their own culture and identity regardless of the influence of outside cultures and the presence of a Communist government. As a people, the Vietnamese still practice ancient traditions and religions regardless of these influences. For example, in a communist nation, one would hardly expect temples and shrines to be populated by priests and disciples who are actively practicing their eastern religions of Confucianism, Taoism, and Buddhism. Yet this is what one sees in Vietnam. The communist nation of China was hardly this receptive to any religion when the author last visited there, and the former Soviet bloc was anti-religious years ago. Yet, Vietnam does have a long tradition of Confucianism, and the Vietnamese people both in Vietnam and here in Southern California live by its principles in general. These principles would include respect for parents, teachers, and elders, minimizing the self for the goodness of the family and society and fulfilling one's obligations to people based on one's status in the family and community (Leung and Boehnlein 1996, 296).

In 1979–1980, when the author was first interviewing Vietnamese individuals and couples in Southern California, "Little Saigon" was just developing into a viable ethnic center for Vietnamese shopping and interaction. Today, it is the main ethnic community for the Vietnamese people. Situated in the city of Westminster, "Little Saigon's" Vietnamese influence radiates out to the surrounding communities of Garden Grove and Fountain Valley where there are restaurants in abundance and Buddhist temples. There the Vietnamese language is reinforced by the spread of markets, shops, and offices where immigrants from Vietnam go on with their day-to-day business. Both the young and the old attend services at Buddhist temples and celebrate important holidays there, like the Vietnamese New Year.

The strong community ties maintain Vietnamese identity through the sharing of a common language and culture. Even with upward mobility occurring with the younger generation, "Little Saigon" is still an urban enclave that is easily accessible for middle- and upper-class Vietnamese working and living in Los Angeles and other areas. Though many Vietnamese are fairly well-assimilated today in the United States, they are not assimilated enough to be marrying outside of their group in large numbers like the Japanese have done.

In an earlier article, Montero saw the Vietnamese refugees as having a good education and some familiarity with the United States culture despite leaving their homeland abruptly. He predicted the Vietnamese would assimilate faster to American society than earlier Asian immigrants because they experienced temporary refugee camp experiences, that provided some post-war stability, and private sponsorships before settling into ethnic enclaves (1981). The private sponsorships dispersed the Vietnamese to diverse non-Vietnamese areas around the nation with economic assistance. However, the existence of "Little Saigon," which is the largest Vietnamese community in the nation, would contest the view that the Vietnamese are assimilating faster than other Asian immigrants to the United States.

## DATA FROM THE PILOT ETHNIC
## RESEARCH TRAINING PROJECT

There were ten Vietnamese Chinese and ten Vietnamese respondents interviewed in 1980 for the author's Pilot Ethnic Research Training Project. As mentioned in chapter 1, this project was designed to train faculty members to do research in ethnic communities so information was collected first that would be useful in training the faculty. This information came from interviews with select members of the Vietnamese community who were from various backgrounds, but who either lived in the community or were very familiar with it. They were asked the same standard questions (the interview schedule can be found in the appendix) that were used with all the ethnic groups about their views on academic research and researchers. Their responses will be summarized below with comments from the author as she analyzes their responses in a broader context.

### Attitude toward the University

The university was regarded very highly by the Vietnamese as a place to gain knowledge and an understanding of many things in life. It was also a good place to reach one's highest educational goals and to develop a professional career. A person with a higher degree would be respected because the bachelor's degree is difficult to achieve in their country. It requires the passing of difficult exams and paying a high tuition. Though the university is an important and respected institution for the community, they are aware that there are prestigious universities, others that are not so prestigious, and some that are more commercially oriented that one would want to differentiate.

These attitudes toward the university are consistent with this population being highly educated when they first came over as refugees. They have also been very upwardly mobile and successful as entrepreneurs in California and continue to place a high value on education similar to other Asian American groups.

## Attitude toward Researchers

In general, the Vietnamese respondents were favorable toward researchers from the university coming to study them in their communities. Some of these individuals took the view that both students and professors would be well-trained and prepared for the task of research and would understand the needs of community members. Even those without much knowledge of community research felt that researchers should be welcome if they are prepared and interested, but professors would be preferred to student researchers in some cases. Since the university people are intelligent and knowledgeable, some respondents would even be happy to provide information about their community or culture. They are also assuming that the research will be of positive benefit to the community, and that the researcher is really interested in learning about their culture and ways, which are little understood by the American people.

However, there was a group of respondents who would be uncomfortable being interviewed by professors or students if they did not know them. They would want to know who the researcher is and his purpose for studying them before they would open up to him and answer questions.

The favorable response of Vietnamese to researchers entering their community goes along with their respect for the university and the high esteem in which they hold professors. Their culture also stresses the importance of hierarchy, so it is not surprising that professors would be preferred over students. In cases where they would welcome researchers, it is in the same vein that they would welcome a high status person coming to their home to make a visit and to do an interview. There also seems to be a certain amount of trust implied in this welcome and the belief that the researcher will help the community and almost serve as a link for them to the wider society that does not know much about the Vietnamese. They are also assuming that the researcher's representation of their culture will be accurate. Since very little has been written about the Vietnamese, until recently, this particular population may not know yet how accurate the research about their community has been.

The more negative comments from Vietnamese respondents show a distrust of the researcher that might be similar to how they would feel about a stranger asking them detailed questions. It doesn't matter if the researchers are professors or students from a university. They must first prove themselves to be genuine and trustworthy before an interview will be granted. One can speculate about the origins of this distrust. Perhaps it is related to the wartime perceptions the Vietnamese may have formed about American soldiers on their territory. Though the Americans were there to prevent the communist takeover of South Vietnam by the North Vietnamese, there is still a lot of negative sentiment toward the American soldiers who bombed villages and tortured villagers. Another possibility is that when the Vietnamese first came over as refugees—and it would be this particular group of respondents—they experienced a lot of prejudice and discrimination from the American public. The Vietnam War had ended only a few years earlier, and the American people still saw the Vietnamese not only as foreigners but sometimes as the enemy who killed American soldiers and set deadly booby traps for them. Thus, even though the Vietnamese had not been here that long when the Pilot Ethnic Research Training Project was going on, some of them may have developed a distrust of Americans and, therefore, researchers, based on negative experiences they have had. This fits with the earlier hypothesis that the more negative historical and relational experiences a group has with the host society, the more distrustful they will be of that group.

## Legitimate Areas of Research

The respondents saw a need for more research that allows the Vietnamese to receive a better education in this country. They wanted to understand university programs better and learn English as a second language so that they could get better jobs and adjust to American culture more easily. They also wanted research done on daily living needs, on family planning and birth control, on health, job training, education, the elderly and facilities for them, and on mental health (especially the traumas of newly arrived refugees). Others wanted to see cultural studies done to promote an awareness of East/West traditions and customs.

It is nice to see that ethnic group members can articulate their problems and needs like these respondents did. It shows that community members are the best people to approach and interview when you want to study them about any topic, including finding out about their daily life and their historical experiences. Their concerns reflect the earlier experiences they had like their need for bilingual education and English as a second language (ESL) classes, which are services that will facilitate their adjustment to American society. Their need for research on mental health is suggesting the desire for services targeting a population that was traumatized during the war, as well as medical services in general that could help with family planning and birth control. Culturally, one can see that the Vietnamese are able to adapt to their new home, and the services they would want are very practical such as job training and education. As recent refugees, they would also want their elders taken care of, which is a family responsibility, but this would require knowledge of other community services. Their desire for more cultural understanding between the East and the West is perhaps related to reducing negative group experiences and perceptions. The high value placed on education by the Vietnamese stands out both as the desired focus for future research on their community and as the source from where research should come.

## Nonlegitimate Areas of Research

For the Vietnamese, asking personal things about an individual, or in a personal way, would not be acceptable when research is done. This applies to anything about oneself or one's family that goes beyond modesty or that deals with a personal problem. One doesn't say anything negative about one's family, such as the existence of a generation gap, because this would harm others. The Vietnamese are very conscious of their family and want to protect them. They would not give out personal information about family members like their being in ill health or about sexual matters, even if it is being requested by medical personnel. One respondent said that he wouldn't mind being asked his income or age but family matters are strictly taboo. If you have personal problems or a crisis, you turn to your own family and relatives to discuss these things. If you cannot resolve them in the family, then you ask a respectable elder in the community for assistance, an individual who is known for providing good counsel. Anyone else would be inappropriate because they are outsiders.

On another note, research should pertain to an area that needs to be studied and not just whatever area is of interest to the researcher. Research instruments should be short and specific so they don't take up too much time. Long and complicated studies or interviews can be viewed as a "waste of time" according to some respondents, while others did not care how long the interview was as long as the research was helpful to the people and tries to identify their needs. However, the questions should be easy to understand and simple so respondents are not confused by them, and the research should be done when there is a need for it in the community and not just at the whim of the researcher.

In analyzing the above information, what is critical here is the importance of the family to the Vietnamese. The family is a very private group, and what takes place within the family is off limits to outsiders. Problems are a source of shame for the Asian family and they can "lose face" or honor if other people knew about them. This is why psychotherapists must be very careful when they see Asian clients and diagnose them, because the client may not return to therapy out of a fear of "losing face" (Kim et al. 2004, 364). This is especially the case with male clients. Losing face can occur because the individual is seeking help outside of the family (which is not culturally acceptable) and is also being diagnosed with a mental illness.

Several cases come to mind for the author, who is a marriage and family therapist in private practice, as well as a sociology professor, that relate to this issue of "saving face." One young Vietnamese male client that she saw was psychotic and needed to be referred to a psychiatrist for medication and further treatment. However, the client refused to see a psychiatrist because he would be labeled mentally ill. He was aware that he had severe problems and thought that medication may help him, but he could not follow through with this referral because (the author suspects) he and his family would lose face. After lengthy persuasion with the client, the author did get the client to agree to see a psychiatrist but only if the psychiatrist was Vietnamese and affordable. The author succeeded in finding such a person for her client and asked him to make an appointment to see the Vietnamese psychiatrist. Because of confidentiality matters, the therapist could not make the appointment for the client. The client did not make an appointment with the psychiatrist, and his argument was that this psychiatrist, who is Vietnamese and works in the Vietnamese community where the client lives, would know about his mental health problems and maybe tell other people about him. Or the community would know about him and his problem because they would see him go into the office. Both situations would make him "lose face." After several unsuccessful follow-ups, the client was never heard from again.

Another Vietnamese client that the author saw was a woman married to an American man. This client was also upset that the author/therapist recommended more prolonged therapy for her. This meant to her that she was mentally ill, and she did not like that conclusion. Though she was not psychotic, she presented with some symptoms that would have required more long-term therapy to eliminate, and the author could only see her for three sessions. The client clearly did not want to see another therapist after the three sessions with the author, so she chose to work hard on her symptoms, instead, and pretty much eliminated them after the first two sessions. Whether or not she remained symptom-free after these sessions is open to debate, but the client did show considerable improvement—enough improvement for the author to be comfortable with terminating her. It is possible that this client wanted to get better so much that she actually did create permanent changes in herself, all so that she would not be diagnosed with a mental illness, which would make her "lose face."

The strong value placed on "saving face" was evident in a study done by N. Mark Shelley on urban Vietnamese refugees in Milwaukee. Even though his study found that the Vietnamese community in Milwaukee was highly fragmented and hardly existed at all, individual Vietnamese and subgroups that lived there were very concerned with saving face. It basically resulted in these individuals limiting or excluding from discussion any negative issues and problems encountered by the community (2001, 485).

Actually, many Asians from traditional cultures would not want their crises resolved by outside mental health professionals. They would prefer the use of an older person in the community, because this is the person who has wisdom and would be neutral. In a hierarchical society where age brings status, either a man or woman could play this role. Many years ago, the author saw a Japanese couple in severe marital conflict knock on her mother's door for counsel over their marital disputes. The author's mother was a good friend of this younger couple, and they trusted her years and knowledge as well as her calmness to bring peace to their household. She must have been effective with this couple, because they came back several times to see her.

## Notification of Research

Most respondents would like to be informed of the research through a notice sent through the mail with the research purpose and topic clearly explained. A formal letter requesting their participation would be appropriate, though some individuals would not mind notification by telephone. By receiving information in the mail, respondents would have time to think about their participation and would be better prepared to respond. The Vietnamese newspaper is another possible source of notification of the research.

## Research Behavior around Respondents

According to respondents, it is very important that the elderly are treated with respect because they have gained wisdom over the years and have more knowledge than the younger members of the community. Therefore, the stranger (researcher) who meets with a Vietnamese family for the first time should introduce himself properly and greet elderly persons first. He should explain his research purpose and politely encourage their cooperation in the study. It is important that he ask permission to interview family members. Prior socializing is important, and the researcher should find out how the individuals would like to be addressed. This is important, because some people prefer to be addressed more formally as Mr. or Mrs. with a surname, while others prefer a more informal approach using their first name, which is less common than using surnames.

Honesty and sincerity in the researcher are important, because individuals may think the researcher is simply another government official questioning them about their status here, and they would be suspicious of him. Along with these qualities, the researcher should also be friendly toward people and have a positive attitude. People do not want to be intimidated by someone who is not friendly, and they will not open up to such a person.

After the elderly are approached by the researcher, he or she can go to the younger members of the family who are treated more informally and with friendliness. If upper class families are being interviewed, they are assumed to be more highly educated and, therefore, are accorded more respect and politeness, though it is proper to treat all men and women with respect, politeness, and friendliness.

The Vietnamese would dislike a researcher who is arrogant and superior. They do not appreciate someone who uses his education to put himself above other people in attitude and manners and acts like "he knows it all." An insincere person would also be disliked because he could mislead them about the purpose of the research. Nor would an insensitive person who cannot see the needs of the community be of much help to them. His lack of concern would be offensive to community members.

When the Vietnamese are being interviewed, they do not appreciate a direct way of being asked questions or having to answer questions right after meeting the researcher. They will answer questions after they have warmed up to the researcher and have socialized a while. Because the Vietnamese are introverted in manners, which is valued in their culture, being direct and extroverted is considered tactless and indelicate. Instead, they will tolerate a wide range of behaviors and display subtle mannerisms, which the Westerner may not understand or even notice because of his more direct approach to people. Vietnamese behavior is usually controlled and patient when the person is interviewed on legitimate subjects of research.

One can see from these responses that the Vietnamese have a hierarchy that determines how people should be treated. Unlike Western beliefs in equality and democracy, people are not treated all the same in Asian cultures. This is neither good nor bad. The hierarchy originally stems from Confucianist beliefs about the proper role of family and community members. Elders are ranked very high as well as highly educated people in this patriarchal culture.

This belief in hierarchy is coupled with the notion that politeness, respect, and friendliness should be an inherent part of interactions between strangers. This insures that roles and relationships will operate smoothly even if there is no equality. Warmth would be appreciated from the researcher because this would mean that he/she cares about the people, and the qualities of sincerity and honesty in the researcher may be important because the Vietnamese know too well the perils of government domination from foreign and domestic (communist) rule, not to mention the insecurities of being in refugee camps and being foreigners in this land.

The most important cultural behavior in the researcher that is desired by the Vietnamese is his/her ability to be indirect in communication style. This may be difficult to do for the American who likes to get to the point and does not have time to socialize with respondents. However, Asians like to be in control of their emotions, and they also want to be read accurately by others. This requires that a stranger take the time to observe nonverbal behavior and be able to read expressions on people's faces. If a person cannot do this, then it is important to spend time getting to know one's respondents better. This is necessary to win their trust, and it helps the respondent to find out more about the researcher and his research interests.

As a therapist, the author works very differently with Asian clients than she does with Western clients. She may offer the Asian clients tea and ask them about their interests and where they are from originally and listen to their comments about objects in her office (home). She will wait until the client brings up the matter that brought them in for therapy and then start asking them questions related to that. With Western clients, she may offer them water or coffee and then go straight to the matter at hand. Along the way, she will gather all kinds of information about the client, so there may be light moments as well as heavier moments. The therapy itself is not really any faster with one type of client or the other. It is just the beginning part that moves along more leisurely with Asian clients because of the indirect style of communication that is used. The author also reads body language and facial expressions, especially the eyes, of Asian clients much more than she does with Western clients because that is the way Asians express their emotions and their pain. The client does not have to say much if it can be read by the therapist. The therapist just needs to check in with the client to see if the message she picks up from him or her is accurate.

## Cultural Customs and Taboos

In this section, Vietnamese respondents mentioned a wide range of cultural customs, superstitions, and taboos. Many of them were stated as "do's and don'ts" for the researcher to observe so they will be summarized that way here.

Do's

1. Leave your shoes at the door before entering a household.
2. Sit where the host directs you to sit.

3. When offered a beverage, that is, coffee or tea, drink it leisurely and finish the drink before leaving the house.
4. Keep a respectable social distance between yourself and the host.
5. Observe the status difference between males and females. Women defer to men and wives are subservient to husbands.

Don'ts

1. Do not lavish admiration on a new baby. If you do, the devils will hear you and steal the child away because it is so desirable.
2. Do not go "Dutch Treat" at a restaurant with other Vietnamese. Either they or you should pay the entire bill. Actually, the one who extended the invitation should pay the whole bill in all politeness.
3. Do not call a person by his first name if he is older than you.
4. Do not give a Vietnamese a cat because it could bring bad luck.
5. Do not wear your hat and shoes in a Vietnamese temple or church. The temple may be public, but as a sacred place, it would uphold tradition more strongly than the home.
6. Do not hand someone a toothpick.
7. Do not refuse tea that is offered by a host or hostess. You must drink the tea even if you don't like it.
8. Do not bring a family a gift that the family could easily buy themselves. This insults their own buying power.
9. Do not break a mirror.
10. Do not touch the top of a person's head. This is demeaning.
11. Do not eat before the elders do.
12. Do not comb your hair at a person's home.
13. Do not overturn musical instruments.
14. Do not beat both sides of a drum simultaneously.
15. Do not eat the fruits in a house or temple that are the worship offering.
16. Do not go to a person's house on the first day of the moon year (Vietnamese New Year's). If you come early during the day, this will affect your daily life for the entire year.
17. Do not accept food from the host too hastily. Adults politely refuse food so that the host can insist that the person take the food. At this point, you can accept it graciously. Accepting food outright is a sign of greediness and bad manners.
18. Do not assume that Vietnamese approve of American customs. For example, dating is not approved of by traditional Vietnamese families. In Vietnamese culture, male/female relationships would not be allowed to develop.

Many of these customs and taboos have to do with politeness and indirectness, which is central to Vietnamese culture. Being patient, reserved, and aware is the message given off by these do's and don'ts. The indirectness is beautifully captured in the statements about food or beverages being served to a guest. One does not hurry about accepting food or drinks, but you must eventually accept the refreshments and partake of them before you leave. Eating carries a lot of norms with it in this culture, from elders eating first, to the sacredness of food offerings that should not be eaten in a house or temple. Maybe Westerners were seen eating this food by the Vietnamese so that they have been concerned about the violation.

The author has visited Vietnamese temples in "Little Saigon" during New Years and there are food offerings in the temple. However, there are also boxes of tangerines in the temple, and the public can take a few tangerines home. Before entering the temple, you must remove your shoes at the entrance, and there are so many shoes there that even an uninitiated observer would know what to do. However, it is possible that some Westerners may think this custom does not apply to them because they are American. That is not the case and they would be violating a cultural taboo.

## Conclusion

These respondents were interviewed in 1980 when they had only recently come to the United States. Therefore, it is not surprising that they retain so much of their ethnic culture and beliefs. Yet, they are also sharing things that even Vietnamese who are more assimilated would agree with today. For example, the Vietnamese do value things about American society, such as education and people associated with the university. They also want their adjustment to American society to be easy, so they would want research done to help them get their needs met as refugees. Well, we now have many services in the Vietnamese community of Little Saigon, such as health and mental health services. However, the Vietnamese culture would still have areas that clash with these services. For example, mental health services were needed for wartime traumas suffered by earlier refugees, but it is possible that many of these refugees were reluctant to receive help because of the cultural belief that negative things about the family should not be shared with outsiders. They believe that one should be very conscious of and protective of the family, and information about ill health in the family or the acknowledgement of personal problems would be inappropriate to share with strangers.

This belief is still very prevalent today as the author can attest to as a marriage and family therapist who has seen Vietnamese clients in her private practice. Younger Vietnamese are just as likely as older ones to not want to go to therapy, especially long-term therapy, because it would be an admission of their having a mental health problem. It would be very shameful if word got out to the Vietnamese community that they were in therapy. Yet, these are clients who could be very much in need of counseling for problems that can be quite severe. If they do come in for therapy, it is reluctantly, and they try to get out of it as quickly as possible. This is the case even if they are seeing an Asian or Vietnamese therapist. As far as research is concerned, these issues and problem areas may never be revealed to a researcher who asks questions about the family.

Because the culture dictates formal and correct behavior with strangers, Vietnamese families as opposed to Western families may require more indirectness and polite socializing to establish rapport and trust. If this is not done properly, research questions may be avoided or responded to incorrectly. Of course, one can tell that rapport has not been established when the respondent or client remains silent and does not convey much information.

## CAMBODIANS

Besides the Vietnamese and Vietnamese Chinese, two other ethnic groups were included in the original study of Southeast Asians. The Cambodians were included in the study because this ethnic group was arriving in significant numbers during the time of this study, and they eventually formed a very large community in Long Beach. Unfortunately, it was difficult to find interviewers for this ethnic group, so information from Cambodian respondents was not available to include in this book.

Today, the Cambodian community is thriving in Long Beach and would be a very interesting group for researchers to study. Cambodians also comprise a large Southeast Asian group in Stockton where the women, especially, have evolved into strong leaders for their Cambodian enclave and in the city itself (Ui 1991). Unlike the other Asian groups, Cambodians are heavily influenced by Northern India. The people speak the Khmer language, and the country is known for its beautiful Khmer temples (Thinh 1979, 2). Buddhism is the major religion of the country, and the people regard their Buddhist priests with the highest respect. At the time of this study, the author was able to interview two Cambodian Buddhist priests, including one who was very old and venerable. They were considered to be part of a very scarce population since the communists killed off the majority of the temple priests when they took over Cambodia. The priests were highly regarded in Long Beach, because they were the moral, spiritual, and psychological leaders of the community.

Even though Cambodian interviewers could not be found for this study, it is very important to use the right type of personnel when collecting data on Southeast Asians. Anthropologists routinely use members of an ethnic community as informants when they do fieldwork with foreign populations or in countries where they are foreigners. This is important because language barriers and trust issues can make it difficult to gather fieldwork data when one is not of the same ethnic background as one's respondents. Even when informants are used, the gender of the informant can make a difference in collecting data, as well as how community members perceive informants.

Bunte and Joseph's 1992 study of a section of a Cambodian community in Long Beach, California, revealed that a team approach to collecting information was useful. This was a high crime area and access to households for interviews was difficult because informants could be perceived as gang members if they were males. That is why the teams included a woman, who was less threatening than a male and was less likely to be suspected of criminal motives. When males were used as informants, a non-Cambodian male was teamed up with a Cambodian male, because a group of all Cambodian males could be perceived as a gang in this area (Bunte and Joseph 1992, 17).

Access can also be affected by trust even when one is with an informant. Bunte's study revealed that knocking on a resident's door was not successful in reaching the respondent in the Cambodian community. If one is a stranger to the neighborhood, residents will not open their door to you perhaps out of fear that you will rob them or report them to the authorities. To solve this problem, Bunte's teams would come to the house during the day when people were more likely to be outside. They would begin a conversation with the resident and then have that person introduce them to their neighbor. This enabled the team to get invited into the homes where they would be offered refreshments and a longer conversation (Ibid., 8).

Fear of how information might be used was another community concern that Bunte's teams discovered when they studied both Cambodians and Hispanic individuals who lived in the Cambodian neighborhood. This fear could affect the accuracy of information given to the research team. For example, a Hispanic family might refer to someone living with them as a visitor rather than a relative or member of a household, because they don't know how the information will be used (Ibid., 15). This is an example of social desirability bias common to survey research.

## THE LAO

The other Southeast Asian group that was part of the study was the Lao. Actually, the Lao people who originally immigrated to the United States from the nation of Laos were comprised of two different groups. There are the general Lao, who are lowland dwellers with a Thai cultural origin, and the Lao Hmong, or mountain dwellers (Thinh 1979, 2). The Hmong people were farmers and livestock breeders in their own country and were accustomed to the freedom that their name implies—Hmong means "free man" (Indochinese Refugee Reports, May 1980, 3). However, the Hmong people were not accustomed to urban ways like the lowland Lao because of their greater isolation from cities and from Western contact. When they first came to the United States, the American public knew little about them, and they knew nothing about American society. What little we knew about the Hmong people was their role in the Vietnam War where they served as mountain guerillas and assisted American soldiers through dense jungle terrain. Because of the heavy sacrifices they made in the war, where many of them died, the United States government acknowledged them by bringing them here for resettlement. The greatest number of Hmong members ended up in California, first in Long Beach and later in the farming communities of the Fresno area.

Though the sample size of the Lao community members who were interviewed in this study was very small, the author decided to include the responses from these five individuals in this book because their culture is so unique, and the population is still little known to the American public. Their responses to the same questions that were asked of the Vietnamese show some similarities to this group but also differences. They will be summarized and discussed in the following paragraphs.

## Attitudes toward the University

The attitude of the Lao toward higher education was very positive with a feeling of respect for the university. The university was considered beneficial as a means of attaining a better job in this country and also a place to acquire knowledge to live a good life. For those who are too poor or too old, it would not be practical for them to go on to college, but sons and daughters would benefit from higher education.

From these comments one can notice that the Lao, like other Asians, see the United States as a highly developed nation with opportunities and resources for upward mobility. Though many of them did not have much education when they first came here, and many of the Hmong women were illiterate, one can see that this group values education—not just for attaining a better job, but also to acquire wisdom. Education bestows status and respect on an individual and also helps the person handle life better, especially in an urban context.

Since these Lao respondents consider themselves to be old when they are in their 50s (because of a shorter life span with this earlier generation), they believe they would not benefit from higher education. They also may not qualify for higher education in our country if they did not complete high school. However, they have optimism for the younger generation to get ahead through higher education. These sons and daughters were working as translators for their parents during the 1980s, and they were an important link to the Western world for them as far as acquiring health and social services for them. Like the children of other immigrant groups, their assimilation to American culture would be much faster than that of their parents, and their longetivity, acquisition of higher education, and ability to get jobs should be much better than in the previous generation.

## Attitude toward Researchers

In general, the Lao respondents had no strong objection to research being done, especially if it benefits the individual or the community in some way. However, all five respondents wanted to know what the research was on, they wanted instructions on how to proceed, and they wanted an explanation of the research purpose. They would feel that the research is all right if it has the backing of some legitimate group like the government, but one respondent had a strong objection to medical research being done in the community because he would not want to be used as a guinea pig.

These responses from the five Lao basically show a positive attitude toward researchers. However, they are qualified in that there is some reservation about research based on how it is being done, who it will serve, who is sponsoring the research, and whether or not it is experimental. The Lao already know the government as a legitimate body because it was a government sponsored airlift that brought them over. They may not know much about the other institutions in our society, but hospitals may be viewed with suspicion, as the final comment indicates.

## Legitimate Areas of Research

Most of the respondents preferred research that deals with solving problems unique to this group, such as refugee adjustment to American society, acceptance by Americans, knowing how to get assistance from the police, knowing how to be protected from crime, danger and accidents, and how to improve the quality of life of the Lao people. The Lao respondents did not object to how much research was done in their community and how long it took to be completed, but they did object to certain areas or topics being discussed. These areas include questions about sex, questions about diseases (i.e., leprosy and scabies—diseases that would reflect negatively on the people), personal questions related to the family (i.e., husband/wife or boyfriend/girlfriend relations, and family finances.

In looking at these responses, it is not surprising to see that the Lao want help with adjusting to American society. They came from rural areas, and they end up in urban areas in the United States that would require a great deal of adjustment for them. When they first came over, the author would see Lao women in traditional clothing sitting on the floor in the hallway of a social service agency. Culturally, they did not think it was inappropriate to sit on the floor, because this is what they may have done back home. Other stories the author heard were more alarming, including women using the toilet to wash their rice, young boys sometimes urinating against a tree in public, young males not being dressed properly when they first arrived in Los Angeles (social workers sometimes had to bring pants to the airport because the young boys were not wearing any), and small children running out into the street and getting hit by cars because they did not know what they were. Los Angeles County can be a very dangerous place for the average American, but can you imagine how much more so it would be for mountain people who do not know what electricity is and do not turn on lights in their home or know how to use appliances? Dressed in foreign clothing and being non-English speaking, they would easily stand out as targets for crime, while their lack of knowledge of modern, urban life would constantly put their lives in danger. Once acculturation settled in, though, these dangers would be less paramount.

The Lao Hmong have adjusted over the years to city life in Long Beach. Today, they are known for their embroidered crafts and textiles with unique designs. A sizeable group of Hmong people, though, found city life very difficult to adjust to, and they chose to be resettled in the farming communities of Fresno where they form a large minority. They would still be traditional in many ways, so the researcher should be discrete in asking questions about areas that they considered inappropriate.

## Behavior around Community Members

The Lao respondents would participate in research in any way, but they would like to deal directly with the researcher. They would want the researcher to have someone in the community speak for him or introduce him to its members before starting the research. Going directly to the people when they do not know him is not appropriate. Once the people know who the researcher is and give their permission to be interviewed, he should then act friendly and helpful. The Lao appreciate it when the researcher is there to help the community in some way, but the help must come from the heart and be genuine.

The Lao stress the idea of making yourself sociable so they know you are a friend. Casual conversation is appropriate in the beginning. After this happens, then the interview can proceed. The people will trust the researcher if he first spends the time to get acquainted with them. Politeness is important as well as being kind to people of all ages. However, the most important thing to observe is proper behavior toward the elderly who should be treated with respect and be approached first when conducting research. The youth must be obedient to parents and should not be addressed except through adults. Men should be approached first, while women and wives should not be visited unless the male is present. The Lao do not like exaggerated behavior or any type of behavior that is out of line with what they have allowed for the researcher. Therefore, the researcher should not do anything beyond what they have approved.

These comments point to the strong norms operating in the Lao culture that determine proper behavior between strangers. Politeness, sociability, and indirect conversation style is the rule similar to the Vietnamese culture. There is also the social hierarchy evident in who to address first and a stronger norm than among the Vietnamese about addressing women and wives and youth.

Like other traditional societies around the world, the Lao would be suspicious of foreigners coming to study them. Here on American soil, though, they are the foreigners, which would make them even more vulnerable than in their own nation. Since they had not assimilated enough to be a part of the larger American society at the time of this study, they would require an informant who could introduce the researcher into their midst.

The Lao respondents show an appreciation for research that is genuinely helpful to them and their community and having a researcher who is like a friend. Trust is important here, and it seems like the Lao had to put a lot of trust in the American government when they were airlifted here during the aftermath of the Vietnam War. They had no idea what they had to adjust to here, but they came over with the blind faith that they would be taken care of and helped. One can see this trust visible in their responses to researchers and research, which, in general, is a little more positive than the Vietnamese responses. The Vietnamese may be seeing Americans as the mighty soldiers who dropped bombs on their country, while the Lao may be seeing Americans as their rescuers.

## Cultural Beliefs and Taboos

The cultural beliefs and taboos of the Lao people that were provided by the respondents will be presented as do's and don'ts, as they were in the earlier section.

Do's

1. Take your shoes and hat off when entering a house.
2. Accept any offering of things such as tea, food, and cigarettes (a refusal means you look down on the people).

3. Be helpful, caring, and cooperative. Treat the family and home with consideration.

Don'ts

1. Do not act disrespectful toward elders.
2. Do not enter a house without permission.
3. Do not conduct research when the husband or male head of the household is not present.
4. Do not interview younger members of the family without the permission of older members.
5. Don't make false promises about research and research results.
6. Don't be misleading about the research, and use the university name to conduct research that does not adhere to stated objectives.
7. Don't walk through a person's house, especially the kitchen.
8. Do not touch a child on the head or embrace him/her.
9. Do not walk in front or in back of a seated person.
10. Do not impose too much of the American-European culture on community members.
11. Do not dress improperly; the researcher should be dressed formally rather than in shorts or other casual attire.

Tradition, honesty, and proper conduct stand out in these responses from the Lao. One gets the notion that acculturation is still very new for them, and they see America as a very foreign place. The casual attire of California is not welcome in the attire of a researcher, and some aspects of American culture are not desirable.

## CONCLUSION

It has been many years since these Lao respondents were interviewed in Long Beach, so it would not be surprising if the young have already been assimilated into American culture. However, assimilation can mean being influenced by negative as well as positive influences, and youth are susceptible to the forces of gangs, drugs, and crime. We have both Vietnamese and Cambodian gangs in Southern California even as these communities maintain their ethnic identity. We also have more Southeast Asian students than ever before who are doing well in colleges and universities around the nation and succeeding in professional careers.

The Lao are still more agricultural than other Asians, but that is not surprising given their background. Their adjustment has been particularly difficult because, culturally, they have been the least westernized of all the recent immigrant groups to the United States. That they have been able to make it in our society is a testament to their strength, courage, and endurance as a people. The author once attended a meeting where several older Lao Hmong women were present. A younger Lao woman who spoke English gave a presentation on the hardships that the Lao women suffered as they tried to adjust to a modern, literate society. After the presentation, I spoke to one of the older Lao women, through the translator, and told her how courageous and strong she was for coming here. The tears that welled up in her eyes said it all. There was so much that she could not tell me, but I was moved by all that was implied.

# Chapter 7

# African Americans

As a racial minority group in the United States, African Americans have been studied longer and more frequently by sociologists than any other ethnic group. The research topics on African Americans have varied from studies on slavery and its aftermath, segregation and desegregation, racism, discrimination, and civil rights, to studies on socioeconomic status and upward mobility, family structure and roles, cultural values, religiosity, deviance, and anything else that a researcher could contemplate. These studies have been insightful as far as showing us how a repressed racial group, who basically had no rights, could emerge from slavery and segregation with new-found rights and upward mobility. However, throughout the history of American society, racial and ethnic groups have been a constant target of prejudice and discrimination by the dominant group, and African Americans have been persistently and severely victimized by discrimination to the point that certain things have not changed for them despite the gains they have made in civil rights and economic advancement.

If we did eliminate some barriers to equal opportunity for African Americans like discrimination in housing, then why are there still so many segregated neighborhoods throughout the nation that are predominately African Americans? They can be found in the South, in urban areas in Los Angeles, and in middle-class suburban areas. Discrimination in employment still exists, especially in blue-collar jobs, which can lead to low income or intermittent employment for African Americans that, in turn, make it difficult to move out of poor segregated neighborhoods. When African American males in these poor neighborhoods become suspects of crime, this leads to a high arrest rate and cases of false imprisonment. Youth in these neighborhoods are mistaken for gang members and end up being homicide cases. Outside of Black areas, African Americans are eyed suspiciously by store clerks in high fashion department stores, who see them as potential shoplifters. These are just some of the myriad of difficulties that plague the life of many African Americans today.

Even when education has been attained, better jobs have been found, and a stable, middle-class lifestyle has existed for quite some time for African Americans, prejudice and discrimination can be noticed in the treatment African Americans receive from others, or in the comments they over-hear, implying a lack of acceptance. This is the burden that many African Americans cannot shake off despite their claim to equal rights. The Civil Rights Movement of the 1960s raised our awareness of White privilege in American society and the discrepancies in treatment between Blacks and Whites. It did not remove the negative stereotypes of Blacks that get reinforced by the media.

How do African Americans respond to unequal treatment and attitudes of prejudice by others? Not being able to trust others would be high on the list of reactions. Living under constant oppression that includes day-to-day discrimination and being treated as invisible can lead to stress, anxiety, depression, frustration, and anger (Weaver 2005, 119). Lack of acceptance and feeling the hostility of others could lead to despair and a turning inward into one's own social group or friends and family. This can result in a strong sense of community even though there is vice and instability in low income areas.

Even though many African Americans have moved up in socioeco-nomic status over the years, the greater number remain in segregated neighborhoods with low income and unequal resources. For those African Americans who have achieved a higher quality of life, they can still distrust other people more than other groups, namely, Whites and Asians, because they experience much more discrimination (Aguilera and Emerson 2005). In low income areas, discrimination can take the form of African American parents' concerns being ignored or minimized by school staff and by their children receiving harsher punishments for the same offenses than non-black children, like receiving suspension instead of detention (Muir, Schwartz, and Szapocznik 2004, 296). Continual forms of discrimination and racism, such as these, make it less likely that African Americans will trust the outsider to be making decisions for them. Higher education has always been valued by African Americans and still is the means to escape poverty and inner city segregation. However, in and of itself, education does not get rid of the discriminatory treatment that leads to in-group/out-group distinctions.

# DATA FROM THE PILOT ETHNIC
# RESEARCH TRAINING PROJECT

Twenty African Americans were intensely interviewed by members of their own racial group in the summer of 1980. These respondents lived in the surrounding communities of California State University–Dominguez Hills in Carson, California. When they answered the questions on researchers from the university doing studies in their community, they were most likely to have had the campus of Dominguez Hills in mind.

## Attitude toward the University

Out of twenty respondents, around half of this sample said that they viewed the university with respect. They considered it a place to acquire skills and academic training beyond an associate of arts level. Some individuals felt that the university was an asset to the community since it serves their area of residence and has graduate programs and a curriculum that is adequate. Some respondents, though, felt that the university should reach out more to other minority groups in the surrounding areas on a more professional level beyond what it has attempted to do.

The other half of the respondents felt displeased with the university because it remained aloof from the people and did not serve their needs. In the case of some individuals, it was seen to be so distant from them that they could not relate to it and didn't know what it was like. The university was remembered by some individuals as a place that catered to the upper-middle class White population from the Palos Verdes area (an affluent neighborhood twenty minutes from campus) and, therefore, was considered to be elitist and unconcerned with minority members. Also, the programs at the campus were not considered to be responsive to the needs of African American students because of this emphasis that was present in the 1980s. As a result, African Americans felt they were not accepted as readily or treated as well as White students.

In analyzing these comments, one can see how African Americans in the low income areas surrounding California State University–Dominguez Hills can feel like they are invisible to the university, even though they value the campus and treat it with respect. These sentiments were also voiced at a time when there were more Whites on campus, some of whom came from the affluent PalosVerdes Peninsula, though the campus was also heavily minority during this time. Today, Whites are a small minority compared to the heavily African American and Latino populations that comprise the majority of students at this campus. It would be interesting to see how much of this alienation still exists today between inner-city African Americans and the university.

The university is still remote from the inner-city, lower-income African American neighborhoods of Compton and Watts, but it is known to them through the students who come from these areas and attend the university. Many of these students will be the first ones in their families to receive a BA, and they rely on financial aid and part-time jobs to help them meet the economic demands of higher education. Despite having a majority of African Americans and Latino students, the university still has not kept up with the needs of minority students as far as hiring more African American and Latino faculty and having programs of study that address their concerns.

## Attitude toward Researchers

For many African Americans, research is highly regarded, but respondents mentioned that they never see any research done in their community nor do they ever participate in research or see its results. Yet, they would like to see more of it done.

Some individuals were skeptical and felt that the research done would be incorrectly interpreted, because it is mainly Whites who do research in their community, and African American community members are not asked to interpret the questions or results of research. Because they hear nothing about the research purpose and results, these individuals do not know who will benefit from the research. They were also critical of any research that ends up stereotyping the people and felt that it was important to have African Americans, rather than Whites, do research on their own community. Yet, they would appreciate any type of research that benefits the community and provides feedback to its members.

Some respondents viewed researchers with respect and felt that when they do come into the community, it is to do something helpful. Some of these respondents had previously encountered a researcher that was helpful to them and treated the people well, and these were the type of researchers that they would welcome back.

One respondent made the comment that certain target groups receive more research attention than others, such as senior citizens and high school students, while other areas are practically ignored. Even more important, the results do not get implemented in the community, which leads some individuals to think that research is just "academic exercises" that are not designed to accomplish anything.

It is from these comments that one begins to understand the lack of trust that African Americans can have toward the majority group. If research leads to stereotyping their group in negative ways, then how can they trust the researcher who would be setting them up for future discrimination? This is why they would prefer an African American researcher in their community rather than a White person. This person would also be more perceptive about the areas that need research attention so that the right groups get targeted for study. Yet, any research that is done by anyone to really benefit the community is welcome.

Based on the above respondents' comments, a number of recommendations can be made:

1. It is suggested that when research is done, the community people are able to participate in the research and see its results as well as help to implement them.
2. Extensive publicity about the research needs to be done so that people know it is being conducted.
3. It is important that research is conducted on topics that serve the needs of the community. Some respondents felt that the researcher comes in without really knowing what the real problems are to correct, therefore, researchers have no realistic solutions to make.
4. Research on those things that show the positive aspects of Black community life would be more appreciated than research on topics that reinforce old stereotypes.

## Legitimate Areas of Research

There were a number of research areas mentioned by respondents that were of concern to them. These included the areas of unemployment, housing, ethnic groups (African Americans and Mexican Americans), retirement and the elderly, shopping centers and markets within the community, education, recreation, health care, child-care facilities for working parents, counseling and social service needs of the community, research on the handicapped (especially on vision and learning disabilities), training program for senior citizens regarding employment opportunities, and politics.

The reasons given for selecting the above areas had to do with the practical concerns of daily living. For example, the research needed on shopping centers was vital, because African Americans in certain communities pay more for groceries and receive lower quality foods than Whites do in their communities. Employment research was needed because there are a lot of African Americans who are not able to obtain jobs.

Education has been cited most frequently by these respondents as an area that needs research. This is because they felt the African Americans were receiving inadequate education, particularly in the lower grades, and they perceived that many young people were not going on to higher education. Research was seen as being needed to identify the reasons for this lack of attendance and inadequate education. Ideas proffered were that the universities may not be offering practical courses that will help African Americans get jobs, or that they may not be responsive to the needs of younger people, many of whom had reading deficiencies. If this is the case, respondents stated that more programs need to be established that will bring the youth to the schools, and the university needs to identify the educational needs of the community.

Housing was another area that was mentioned as needing research. This is because African Americans were seen as having had a problem finding housing in the past, and when they get displaced from neighborhoods, they have no place to go. Transportation, too, was perceived by respondents as inadequate since many people are not able to get to places where they need to go. A suggestion was made to institute a new system, maybe the "Red Car" (street car) once again, to meet their transportation needs. Recreation was considered important for the same reason; it is currently inadequate in the communities where people live, and parents must take their children to other cities for things such as movie theaters.

Lastly, political research was considered important because there is a need to seek alternatives to current government practices in the community. Many traditional means of serving the people were not perceived as working. Research, according to one respondent, is valued when it solves problems relevant to the people and when there are resources to implement the recommendations of the study. Social action impact research was suggested by this person because it is studying the conditions that exist before a program is implemented, and because it will identify the needs and concerns of the community.

The value of these comments from African American respondents is that they know what the problems are in their community, and these problems are different from what academicians would consider problems for research. Yet, the two views of problems may be related. The respondents are identifying practical problems that affect the quality of life in their community like inadequate recreation facilities, child-care needs, lack of training programs for the unemployed, and poor quality shopping centers and markets. The lack of adequate resources in the community can lead to the problems that researchers may want to study such as crime, gang behavior, teen pregnancies, and single-parent families. If researchers helped the community solve some of their practical problems, then they could minimize the problems that make the headlines in the African American community and at the same time erase some of the negative stereotypes about this ethnic group.

## When Research becomes a Nuisance

Most of the respondents felt that research could not be a nuisance to them because there was so little research done in their community. Nobody really studies them and their needs; in fact, the respondents felt that they were more often ignored than studied by those in higher education. According to the respondents, any research that helps the community and dispels some of the myths about African Americans would be appreciated; furthermore, any research that is good would not be a nuisance no mater how much of it is done. Some respondents felt that community members from areas like Compton, that receive too much study on the same topics repeatedly, could eventually become annoyed; but, if the researcher knows the community fairly well and the people are allowed to have input into the study, this reaction should be minimized.

Some respondents felt that research is a nuisance if it invades their privacy. Questions that ask them about their income is an example, because it seems to reflect more the researcher's curiosity than a research concern. Also, if the researcher picks the wrong time of the day to do his interviewing, this could be a nuisance to some people. People can also be suspicious of strangers in some communities; therefore, the researcher needs to explain his purpose so he does not intrude upon their privacy and human rights. Of course, if he does do research that infringes upon their rights or makes them feel psychologically uncomfortable, this would be unacceptable.

According to respondents, research should be on topics relevant to the people and these topics should deal with their needs. Furthermore, the people should see the results of research. Many individuals would like to know what the researcher has found out about them, and they get very frustrated when they are interviewed repeatedly but never know what conclusions were made by the researcher or what changes will come about as a result of the research. They feel that the researcher should be aware that he is a guest in the community and not do research merely to impose his own values on the people. He should listen to what they identify as the problem and use the perspective of the people to identify solutions; otherwise, he will be a nuisance.

These respondents are making a good point about research. Research isn't a nuisance to them because nobody comes out to study them unless they, themselves, are the problem. Either they are invisible or the neighborhood is so bad that no one would want to come there and study them. If researchers do come out to study them, it may not be in ways that serve the community or benefit the people. This may be why the results do not get shared with the people after they are interviewed, leaving them with a feeling of powerlessness to bring about beneficial changes in the community. It must be a nuisance to have a researcher bother them at the wrong time of day, intrude on their privacy to ask personal questions, and then take off without any follow up plans that reveal an interest in their community.

## Participation in Research

All of the respondents wanted to be informed about the research proposal, topic, and/or results through such means as local newspapers, the media, letters, flyers, corner posters, newsletters, phone calls, and by word of mouth. They all wanted to participate in the research in some way as well. Responses varied from wanting to be interviewed to describing or interpreting the results of the research findings, interviewing respondents, and facilitating the research by introducing the study to church and community groups. Some individuals wanted to participate in the research from the very beginning, and a number of people wanted to know everything about the research, including the qualifications of the researcher and the methodology used. They would welcome a thorough introduction of the research to the community, which could be done at organizational meetings or church group meetings that are attended by a number of people active in the community.

Some respondents did not want to participate in the research if they were not informed of the results or if the research was not in an area of interest to them. They preferred the research to be announced before interviewers came in to start the study so that the people are informed ahead of time. A further suggestion was made to train community members to do the research rather than just having students do it.

From these responses, one can see that African Americans have a social network in the community that could be used to good advantage if they are consulted thoroughly about the research project. They know how to facilitate the gathering of data and would be willing to participate in a number of ways that could be useful to the researcher, that is, disseminating the results of the research and introducing the study to others at large gatherings. At the same time, they would want to be informed about the research through as many different ways as possible so the entire community has knowledge of it. An awareness of the research even before it is started is important as a sign of courtesy. It is giving people proper notification of an event and allowing the community members to prepare for it.

## Things That Would Offend the People

Many respondents objected to professors and researchers defining the problems of community members for them and then proposing solutions. They resented this because the researcher is imposing his values and perceptions on them and is not prepared to listen to what the people regard as problems. Many researchers are viewed as being uppity and elitist when they place themselves on a pedestal and remain apart from the community. This makes them socially distant from the people and remote from their interests and needs. Thus, they end up assuming that something is wrong with the people psychologically, when the problem is more external.

To others, it is the type of attitude the researcher has that is most offensive. They would not like a person who is patronizing and likely to leave the community with the same erroneous knowledge of the people with which he came in. Some referred to this attitude as being prejudiced or having cultural biases. To others, insincerity or dishonesty on the part of the researcher would be the worst offense. They feel the researcher should not conceal true findings or act inconsistently with what he said about the research, nor should he violate individuals' confidentiality or privacy.

Unlike newly arrived ethnic groups who would be offended by cultural violations, African Americans feel the greatest offense from researchers would be their treating African Americans in a negative way. This is not surprising given a history of discrimination that African Americans have experienced from the society at large and over many, many years. It also raises the issue of trust between African Americans and Whites. Can they trust a White researcher to really know what their problems are? Too often, African Americans have been blamed for their problems. Will they get treated in a fair and just way without prejudice or negative attitudes? Or is the researcher coming in to reinforce a stereotype about them or to just take advantage of them by getting their research needs met without consideration for what the community needs? Trust requires positive interaction before it can be established. Researchers would have to get to know the people and learn about them in a myriad of ways. By doing so, they will appear less distant and elitist and more in tune with the community.

## Expected Behavior toward Community Members

No matter what age group or social group the researcher is dealing with, respondents felt that he should treat everyone with respect and dignity and just be himself. Members of the African American community do not appreciate insincere behavior and are very perceptive of what others think and feel about them. Their awareness of White attitudes has developed over many years of careful observation, according to one respondent, and they are very sensitive about how they are treated and regarded by others. They would prefer that the researcher show some respect and even humility toward them since he is privileged to have their cooperation. If he has compassion and understanding, that would be even better.

A few respondents felt that in the case of children, the researcher should develop a different approach to asking questions, but the treatment should be the same as for adults. He just has to put himself in their place to know how they would like to be treated, and flexibility is important so that the researcher can assess each situation differently and behave accordingly.

When first meeting community members, a number of individuals wanted a proper introduction made where the researcher identifies himself and the nature of his research. Politeness, on his part, and consideration of other people's feelings and needs were considered important, and a friendly face was felt to be more appreciated than a straight and solemn one. Some respondents would want to be properly addressed by the researcher, so he should find out what titles and forms of address to use with community members, that is, Miss, Doctor, or Reverend.

Other things respondents considered important were learning how to listen to the respondent, which again is a sign of courtesy, and learning the language of the people. This latter implies knowing their social cues and behavior patterns as well as what is verbally communicated.

These comments from respondents say it strongly and clearly that how they are treated by researchers is critical to their cooperation and dignity. From learning how to address African Americans using formal titles, to listening well to them as they tell their story, is important in this treatment of the African American respondent.

Demeanor is also important in the researcher since respondents do not want an inaccessible person. Though the researcher could be very academic, he/she should still be friendly, polite, sensitive, respectful, and adaptable. Nonverbal communication can be as important as verbal communication, so being perceptive and aware of the listener's nuances is another important skill to acquire.

## Cultural Beliefs and Traditions

Other than certain foods and strong ties to religion, respondents were not able to identify too many things that made them stand out from the majority group. One respondent mentioned a respect for the elderly, superstitions, and the tradition of offering food to guests, but most of the respondents found it difficult to identify beliefs and cultural customs that were unique and specific to their group.

## CONCLUSION

Many years have gone by since this data was collected on African Americans in their community. Would their responses be different today to research being conducted in their community? I don't think so. It would be wonderful to alleviate the conditions that lead to distrust between racial groups, but this book can only point out its continued existence and through these limited number of responses from African Americans show how it can be minimized in their community.

According to Michael Welch and others, "Social trust is the mutually shared expectation, often expressed as confidence, that people will manifest sensible and, when needed, reciprocally beneficial behavior in their interactions with others" (2005, 457). It is a way to believe that relationships will be reliable in fulfilling needs. When trust does not exist, cooperation is less likely and social solidarity between groups breaks down (Welch 2005, 463). With a long history of experiencing the prejudice and discrimination stemming from societal-entrenched racism, African Americans' ability to trust the majority group could only happen slowly and through positive reinforcement from the majority group.

One way that this can happen is to continue to do more ethnographic research in African American communities, since this is a more in-depth way of acquiring data than surveys, and it requires more one-on-one interaction. Another way of connecting with the community is to use focus groups to identify ethnic group concerns that may lead to an intervention program that will serve the needs of this community. This was done in Georgia where the Center for Family Research at the University of Georgia formed partnerships with representatives of rural African American communities. Using focus groups, researchers were able to develop an intervention program that identified critical problems in the community and ways to delay the onset of these problems (Murry and Brody 2004). These research efforts would be a way to begin building up a trust that is sorely lacking between African Americans and the dominant society. Hopefully, these efforts can multiply and be good models for interracial and interethnic cooperation.

# Chapter 8

# Japanese Americans

## ASIAN AMERICANS

In this chapter, the term "Asian American" will refer to people from the East Asian nations of China, Japan, Korea, and the Philippines. These nations are close to each other, and, with the exception of the Philippines, have influenced each other culturally, socially, and politically.

China's ancient influence on Japan can be seen in the introduction of Confucian values to Japan and the characters of Japanese writing. Koreans also have had the Confucianist influence from China, but they have been dominated by Japan for many years before and during World War II and have been exposed to Japanese language and culture as a result of this domination. The Philippines were a colony of Spain for centuries before they were occupied by the United States and later by the Japanese during World War II. Their indigenous culture shows the stronger influence of Spain through the Catholic religion and the use of Spanish names. While each of these nations is unique in history and immigration to the United States, it is their experience here that becomes significant in understanding how they have been lumped together as a racial group by the dominant society.

The Chinese were the first East Asian group to arrive in America, and they were the first group to experience the prejudice, discrimination, and racism that would later materialize with the other Asian groups, though not to the same extent. Though they began arriving in the 1800s, their numbers were small, and their growth rate was kept minimal due to exclusionary practices and laws. This resulted in a shortage of women and the denial of naturalization rights that prevented the development of a second generation of native-born Chinese Americans or a group of Chinese with American citizenship (Gonzales 1993). Their exploitation as laborers in the gold mines, railroads, and laundry work and their segregation in Chinatowns resulted in the preservation of language, culture, and a strong sense of community since these things were necessary for survival in a hostile environment.

Today, the Chinese are the largest Asian American group in the United States. They are spread out over the United States, though their historical Chinatowns still remain in Los Angeles, San Francisco, New York, Boston, Oakland, and many other places. Known for settling in the West, originally, their population has increased due to the passing of the Immigration Act of 1965. Now this ethnic group consists of old immigrant families connected with Chinatowns, new urban professional immigrants, working class immigrants, and Chinese Americans of many different generations in the United States. The foreign-born population is more noticeable than the "American-born" Chinese because of the factors associated with exclusion mentioned earlier and the large recent waves of Chinese immigration since 1965 (Glenn and Yap 2002, 145–47).

The Korean American community in the United States has also been a product of the 1965 Immigration Act. However, before 1965, Korean immigration to the United States was furthered by the Korean War in 1950 when large numbers of orphans and Korean women married to U.S. servicemen were allowed to come over (Min 2002, 194). Today, this population is growing rapidly, is heavily concentrated in southern California, and is visible in terms of the many Christian-denomination churches that bear Korean lettering.

It is well-known that Korean adjustment to the United States has been hindered by many individuals lacking English skills. Though highly educated with professional backgrounds, many Koreans have had to go into self-employed service jobs, from running mini-markets and restaurants to gas stations and dry cleaners. They usually set up small family businesses in urban, minority areas where they can clash with African Americans, like in Los Angeles. Though these clashes have lessened over the years, the frustrations of being over-skilled and working in low-income neighborhoods could add to assimilation and acceptance difficulties.

Like the Chinese and Koreans, Filipino immigration increased dramatically as a result of the Immigration Act of 1965. Before that happened, Filipino men came over as farm workers in the 1920s and experienced racial violence as they competed with White workers for jobs that became scarce during the depression (Gonzales 1993, 186). Known for their military service, Filipino men used this route as a way of getting U.S. citizenship both before and after World War II. Today, there are many professionals that come over from the Philippines and most noticeable are the physicians and nurses. The lure of coming to America has resulted in the Filipino population being the second largest Asian American population in the United States. Many of these recent immigrants speak Tagalog and maintain Filipino cultural values related to family, food, and religion.

Though these Asian groups have different cultures and unique immigration experiences, they have some similarities to each other and with the Japanese Americans that will be highlighted in this chapter. They have gone through varying degrees of discrimination and racism because of their skin color and other facial features, and these experiences have made them closer knit as ethnic groups. Cultural traits they may hold in common are interdependence and affiliation, a hierarchical family structure based on male dominance (though Filipino sex roles are more egalitarian than the other groups), respect for elders, harmony and balance in one's life, and religious spirituality (Weaver 2005, 169–72). As one example of an Asian American group that has gone through restrictive immigration laws, as well as incarceration during World War II, the Japanese Americans show in-group solidarity despite being highly assimilated and middle class. Their story follows.

## INTRODUCTION TO JAPANESE AMERICANS

Who are the Japanese Americans? Are they like other immigrant groups who found their way to the United States and then began the process of cultural assimilation that would make them lose their language and other group characteristics? The answer would be yes and no. Though many Japanese Americans no longer live in a Japanese community and do not speak the language of their ancestral group, they still stand out by group identity and by some cultural features that are unique to this ethnic group alone. The most noticeable feature is their reference to each other by generation here in the United States.

Takagi describes how two historical periods have produced three birth cohorts and kinship-defined generations of Japanese Americans—the Issei, who are first generation in the United States, the Nisei, who are second generation by birth, and the Sansei, who are third generation by birth. Because most marriages of Issei took place from 1907 to 1924, they were able to produce a significant number of second generation Nisei just before World War II. The Nisei marriages, in turn, occurred mainly during the war and early postwar years so that they were able to produce a concentration of Sansei children between 1945 and 1960. The Sansei's children would be called the Yonsei, or fourth generation Japanese, and they would be born after the 1960s and 1970s (2002, 165).

What do we know about the Yonsei? Actually we do not know a whole lot about this group, but one thing that is evident is that many of them would be mixed ethnically and racially. This is because there was a high rate of inter-marriage with the Sansei generation and the women, especially, were more likely to marry outside their ethnic group than the men. Beginning since the 1960s, this rate in California was close to 50 percent (Kikumura and Kitano 1973). This raises the question of what happens to the Japanese family when there is so much out-marriage (Takagi 2002, 175).

It is possible that the identification of Japanese Americans by gen-eration would stop with the Sansei, or it is possible that a small group of Japanese American Sansei couples who have produced an even smaller Yonsei generation would continue with the idea of maintaining generational continuity through naming cohorts by generation. These Yonsei, in turn, could produce an even smaller fifth generation cohort, though the author has not heard much about this generation, and it may be very difficult to identify such a cohort once it gets too small. However, it is interesting to know that such a group could exist and have some unique cultural characteristics that would be worth examining.

Another cultural feature that would be unique to Japanese Americans is their cohort group connections that show up as friendship circles or social networks. It doesn't matter what generation of Japanese we are talking about, Japanese Americans tend to hang out with other Japanese Americans in social circles that could include other Asians as well. This phenomenon was noted by the author in her published dissertation back in the early 1970s when she studied the Sansei (Hosokawa 1978), and it still exists today. Other ethnic group members also hang out together but with the Japanese, it is a cohort phenomenon, and it can be extreme enough to show up as tightly-knit cliques. Cliques are very exclusive and tend to keep out other people. Individuals who are trying to join the group can feel themselves being snubbed or ignored by the clique. An example of this comes to mind.

Several years ago, the author attended a fundraising luncheon with a Chinese American girlfriend. This friend was an attorney working for a Japanese American law firm, and this firm had bought out a whole table at the luncheon. The friend's husband, who was Caucasian, refused to go with her to the luncheon because he did not like this particular group. He could not explain it, but he just did not like the way he was treated by this group. When the author went to the luncheon, she could understand why the husband did not like this group. It was your classic case of an Asian clique that included mainly Japanese Americans and some Chinese Americans. The author could feel herself being ignored by the members of the clique who only talked with each other and not to her. Only one Japanese American male would talk with her at the table, but he was more separated from the rest of the group. As others have testified when trying to join a clique, one can experience an uncomfortable feeling of being excluded or snubbed by the group.

Now, these individuals were third-generation Japanese or Sansei, and the author's earlier dissertation study, where she noticed clique behavior, was also of Sansei who were students at UCLA. Perhaps this generation was as much into cliques as other cohorts of Japanese Americans, though Kitano only mentioned that the Nisei, like the Issei, have constructed an elaborate network of cliques and organizations (1969, 140). Maybe it was their way of maintaining ethnic identification through tightly-knit social networks, when cultural traits were quickly disappearing as a result of assimilation for this generation. This was the author's conclusion from her dissertation study (Hosokawa 1978). In this sense, clique behavior is not necessarily negative in that it is maintained for group cohesiveness purposes and can be seen as a cultural trait that endures long after its survival function has been served.

It is possible that with so much intermarriage going on with the Sansei generation, cliques are a way to preserve ethnic group ties in the same way that Nisei parents formed tight bonds as a cohort to handle post-World War II prejudice and discrimination. Like their Issei parents, the Nisei would know firsthand about prejudice and discrimination, because they went with their parents into America's relocation centers during World War II or they were born in these concentration camps.

The internment of Japanese Americans during World War II is a historical experience unique to this group alone. Though Japanese immigrants were targeted by discriminatory immigration laws since the early 1900s, and anti-Japanese sentiment existed with the growing economic success of Japanese laborers and farmers, it was the mass evacuation of more than 110,000 people of Japanese ancestry into relocation centers in the United States that was the most negative and harmful act of discrimination toward these people. These individuals were not accused of any crime, and 70,000 of them were American citizens, which raises the question of why this evacuation was necessary (McLemore 1991, 218). Not only did this action take away the freedom of the Japanese people, but it ruined their economic gains and undermined their families. Some people would say that this is what was intended to happen—to diminish a group that was becoming a threat to the dominant society because of economic success.

Though World War II happened in the 1940s, it wasn't too long ago to be forgotten by current generations of Japanese Americans. Many families lost everything during relocation and had to start all over again once the war was over in a society where Japanese were not accepted by many American people. Discriminatory post-war practices prevented many Issei males from finding suitable jobs or living in neighborhoods of their choice. Many Japanese families were destitute during these years. Their Nisei children suffered from discriminatory actions by teachers and negative stereotyping by other students and children in their neighborhoods. Parental authority, which was undermined by the relocation experience because of the regimentation of camp life (Takagi 2002, 172), diminished further as Nisei teenagers became more quickly assimilated into American society than their parents and later became very upwardly mobile.

Since this is a book on building trust, one can surmise that the 1940s was a period of great distrust between the Japanese and the American society. The distrust probably went both ways, since being interned does not make you trust the government or country that takes away your freedom, and those on the outside of the camps could assume you are not to be trusted because you are locked up. Many of the Issei have died now, but the Nisei who were in the camps remember their experience, Their children, the Sansei, know their story, and the Yonsei have heard it from their parents and from the textbooks and media. Those who were interned at Manzanar in the Owens Valley of southern California can go to this site and get the story again from the museum that was built on this former camp. Or they can go to the Japanese American National Museum in Los Angeles to receive a wider coverage of the internment experience.

The $20,000 reparation check paid by the United States government to the Japanese survivors of the camps tried to compensate for some of the economic losses the Japanese people suffered. The apology from the U.S. government that it had erred in its decision to relocate so many Japanese people was probably more significant as far as raising the dignity of the people.

Would these measures lead to greater trust between the Japanese and other Americans? Since the end of World War II, Japanese Americans have made so many economic and educational gains that they were described as being a "model minority." Alas, the word "minority" will always keep you down! As a stereotype, the "model minority" concept only implies that the Japanese Americans have not gained equality. Still lumped together with other minorities, which is a subordinate status, Japanese Americans are now perceived as being a "good" minority. They don't rock the boat, they don't protest this inequality publicly, and they don't demonstrate through marches. This "be good" perception of a minority group fits well with patronization. It does not fit the reality of ethnic group survival in a hostile society. Nor does it imply trust.

Japanese Americans are still insular as a community despite cultural assimilation and intermarriage. As long as they look different from the dominant group they will be perceived as a minority group. Even the Sansei and Yonsei, who are clearly American in their basic values and traditions, will be approached by strangers as an ethnic person first and perhaps as someone from Japan. Proving that one is equal to others by economic and educational achievements does not change the perceptions of people toward ethnic members that are based on skin color and physical features. This is why a level of distrust can exist between people. This distrust can make Japanese Americans more oriented toward their own ethnic group, and it can make the dominant group still suspicious of a Japanese American or curious of members of this group. An example of this suspiciousness toward a Japanese American is when an older American male who fought in World War II tries to test the loyalty of this Japanese American (the author) by saying, "Which side are you on?"

Japanese Americans have had to adapt to an uprooting relocation experience, to a hostile society after the camps, and to their cultural loss with the assimilation of younger generations. Yet, the earlier social contacts do remain strong among Japanese Americans in spite of their past history or maybe because of it. It was mentioned earlier that Japanese Americans hang out with other Japanese Americans. Well, there is another way that they make contact with other members of their own ethnic group and this is in the selection of service providers in the community. Japanese Americans tend to use other Japanese Americans when they choose a doctor, dentist, gardener, pharmacist, optometrist, and for other services. The author is a good example of this practice. She has had a Japanese American general practice doctor, a gynecologist, optometrist, acupuncturist, and even a chiropractor. Her family members use Japanese dentists and go to a Japanese-owned supermarket. Whenever possible, the goal is to find a Japanese service provider first before settling for anything else. This is an interesting way to see trust within one's own community.

The author is aware that members of other ethnic groups or Americans may say they prefer an Asian doctor or dentist, too, so it is not just the Japanese that trust these providers for their service and performance. Historically, Japanese Americans have gone into the medical and dental professions in large numbers because they were trying to regain their loss of finances and dignity after the relocation experience. The medical fields were easier to get into through higher education than other jobs, and they were considered prestigious and lucrative professions. With enough Japanese Americans in the field of medicine who were hardworking and competent, it would not be surprising that other groups would know about them and use their services. Yet, this is different from the trust that occurs from a sense of community. Japanese Americans not only use these professionals because they are competent and skilled but also because they usually get better service from them than from non-Japanese service providers. They also feel more comfortable around professionals of their own ethnic group and feel a sense of kinship with them through sharing a common history and culture.

One can go deeper with this sense of trust among Japanese Americans. Perhaps it goes back to the concentration camp experience of Issei and Nisei where the family was less pronounced than the ethnic group. These similarly treated individuals would have formed a community under duress and forced relocation. Under these circumstances, trust may have been essential for survival, even though there were strong differences in the camp inmates' responses to detention with some favoring militant protest and others wanting accommodation (Miyamoto 1973, 29).

Yet, some of this trust would be cultural, with honesty playing an important part in people's belief that others can be trusted when they are from your same ethnic group. The author can remember an incident that relates to this trust based on the honesty principle. In her younger years, she started taking judo lessons and needed to buy a judo uniform which she found at a Japanese-owned sporting goods store in Gardena, California. When she was waiting in line to buy the judo uniform, she noticed a sign by the cash register that said, "No credit cards." The author told the cashier, who looked Nisei, that she did not have enough cash to pay for the uniform and only had her credit card. The Japanese American woman at the counter said it was okay. Though they didn't take credit cards from other people, she would make an exception in this case. The author took this to mean that it was because she was Japanese that her credit card would be accepted, and the woman could trust her.

Another example of this trust based on honesty can be seen in a group context. The author has gone to social events at Japanese gatherings and sat at tables with other Japanese Americans. When she was with a group of all women at one event, none of whom she knew before this event, she got up to leave the table to go to the ladies room. The Japanese American woman sitting next to her immediately said that the author should leave her purse with her, and she would watch it. The author trusted her completely with her purse just as this woman would have trusted the author with her purse. The author, who is Nisei, knows that this woman can be trusted because she is Japanese and, therefore, honest.

In Japanese culture, one is taught to be honest at an early age. For example, the author learned honesty the hard way by telling her mother a white lie as a child. She discovered that a white lie is still a lie, and it is forbidden in Japanese culture. If the Japanese people are not allowed to lie, then one grows up believing that they can be trusted. This would be true especially with the Issei and Nisei generations. This cultural belief in honesty would make it worthwhile for Japanese Americans to stay in contact with others of their same ethnic group. They may not be able to trust other groups based on how they were and still are treated by them, but they usually could predict the behaviors of their own group members. Even though honesty is not a cultural norm specific to the Japanese people, Kitano would say that norms are very real in the behavioral sense in that they are part of the set of messages that Issei pass down to Nisei and Nisei pass down to Sansei (1969, 101).

There is also a sense of pride that Japanese Americans have about their ethnic group, even though individuals may be assimilated to a greater or lesser extent. This is another way that one can see a sense of community among Japanese Americans that would reinforce their inner group trust and outer group distrust. Japanese Americans like to support their community by cultural or recreational events that bring large groups of people together. They are generous in their donations to these events and in their participation and attendance at the events. These events include the Issei/Nisei picnics that used to be held in Los Angeles, the Buddhist Temple carnivals in cities throughout Southern California, community beauty pageants, and the Nisei Week Parade that is still a long-held tradition in Los Angeles. This pride is also manifested in the Japanese American associations that have a long history in this country. Kitano states that the Issei created the Japanese Association when they first came here to help them protect their community and serve the needs of their people, while the Nisei organized the well-known Japanese-American Citizen's League in the 1920s to continue with this function of protection and service to the Japanese people (1969, 81–83). Over time, each of these associations became less influential as the Japanese community went through changes and the people became more assimilated. However, a third Japanese organization has emerged in recent years and it is gaining in membership and popularity. This is the Go For Broke Educational Foundation based in Gardena, California, that was started as a fledgling group and developed a momentum that made it quite strong today.

As a Sansei-run organization, the Go For Broke Educational Foundation supports the legacy of Japanese American World War II veterans and pays homage to them in ways that raise their visibility in American society. For example, by raising money through fund-raising events, the organization has been able to erect a monument to these soldiers in Little Tokyo, the Japanese community in downtown Los Angeles. The organization's current mission is to collect the oral histories of the remaining veterans so that they will be preserved for future generations of Japanese Americans and so that they can educate the public about their exploits. The popularity of this organization can be seen in the high attendance of Japanese Americans and others at their annual luau, which keeps getting larger every year.

In conclusion, it is interesting to see how a highly-assimilated ethnic group can still have a strong ethnic identity. It is the author's belief that this ethnic identity has been maintained by both subtle cultural and historical factors. These forces have lead to a strong in-group trust when it was difficult to trust out-groups. Japanese Americans may be like other Americans culturally, but they stand out by their skin color and physical features. This makes them easily identifiable as an ethnic group. Their traditional communities still exist and attract tourists, including the Japanese from Japan and Japanese Americans, but most of the Japanese people live outside of these "Little Tokyos" as they blend in with other Americans. Yet, they come together for community events like the Nisei Week Parade in downtown Los Angeles or the annual luau of the Go For Broke Foundation. In this sense they are still a community in spirit and in the support of community activities. This is something that has not changed over the decades regardless of which generation of Japanese predominates in society.

## DATA FROM THE PILOT ETHNIC
## RESEARCH TRAINING PROJECT

Twenty-two Japanese Americans completed questionnaires or were interviewed as part of the author's research project in 1980. These respondents lived in the surrounding communities of California State University–Dominguez Hills. The questionnaires produced information on a number of areas related to how research should be done in the Japanese American community. This data will now be analyzed based on the perspective presented above on how the ethnic group has evolved over time.

### Attitude toward the University and Researchers

The Japanese American respondents as a whole had a high regard for the university. This is not surprising given that many of them had reached middle-class status through attaining higher education. Compared to the other ethnic populations studied, though, they were more selective in awarding a university their respect. They would have higher respect for the more prestigious universities in the area such as UCLA or USC or for a department at a college based on its reputation.

Their responses toward researchers from the university coming into their community showed more variations. For example, some respondents would welcome any researcher from the university doing research on any subject, but they would receive the professor more warmly than the student. Others would be suspicious of the professor because he may be doing research for his own personal benefit and doing it on a topic of no value to Japanese Americans. They would trust the student more because at least he is doing a class assignment and must get a grade or units for it.

Other individuals would be cautious about the type of research being done and would not want to participate in anything that would not benefit them or that they considered "worthless" scientifically. This coincided with the response of other respondents who said they would be more receptive toward a researcher who is sincerely interested in the betterment of the community and who shows respect for the people he is interviewing or observing.

Some respondents would regard the researcher negatively because he is a stranger or an outsider to the community. If he were introduced properly to community members, that is, through their friends or relatives, he would receive a better welcome. One respondent thought it might be a good idea to have the researcher announce his project in the Japanese newspaper so that the community is alerted to it, or he could drop off his business card and other documents explaining his research purpose before beginning the project. This would make his entrance into the community easier. A number of individuals also felt that the researcher should be Japanese if he is going to interview older or more traditional community members. Lastly, there were a number of individuals that highly respected research and felt it should be done, but they did not want to be bothered by an interview.

The variety of these responses could indicate the different degrees of assimilation found among Japanese Americans. For example, those who are more traditional would prefer that researchers approach the older generation differently than the younger generation or would receive the professor more warmly than the student because of his higher status. The more traditional or older respondents may also require more formal introductions before accepting a researcher into their home. Yet, there is also a concern to have research benefit the community and this is where the professor may not be trusted if he was more concerned about his own grant topic and getting his grant refunded than the betterment of the community. A project could be "worthless" to the Japanese even though it may be of interest to the professor, and the respondents would not be receptive to such a person or project. Even though many Japanese Americans are quite assimilated, they may still see themselves as part of a community, and this is where in-group/out-group differences may be evident. The researcher could easily be perceived as someone who is outside the group and not able to identify with the concerns of Japanese Americans. Therefore, he is not to be trusted until they get to know him better.

## Legitimate Areas of Research

Legitimate areas of research were identified mainly in terms of the needs of particular segments of the community, such as the elderly or one's own needs and interests. The needs, of course, were subject to variation depending on changing circumstances in a person's life or changes taking place in the community. Examples of community needs might be low-income housing for the elderly, recreational facilities for lower-income youth, and mental health facilities for those requiring such services.

Individual needs for research or areas of research interest covered a number of different topics. They included the following: ethnic identification, changes in marital roles, receptivity toward family counseling and other therapeutic services, extended family networks, generational differences, spouse battering, child abuse, drug abuse, medical research (ulcers, allergies, multiple schlerosis), the elderly Nisei, physical longevity and generations, bilingual education, historical studies, interethnic marriages, convalescent homes for the elderly, fourth generation studies (Yonsei), and changes in residential patterns.

One can see from these responses that Japanese Americans do not have the strict cultural taboos that other traditional immigrant groups may have. Therefore, what they would consider as legitimate areas of research would have more to do with what interests them or would serve the needs of the community rather than what is acceptable or unacceptable as research topics. This reflects the higher level of assimilation of this small sample of respondents.

However, the research topics of interest to this population reveal some of the contemporary issues they are dealing with, such as child abuse, interethnic marriages, convalescent homes for the elderly, fourth generation studies, generational differences, changes in marital roles, and receptivity toward family counseling. Many of these issues from the 1980 study are certainly relevant in our society today, and the author has certainly seen these problems in her private practice as a marital and family therapist. Another thing that is interesting about these research topics is that they show what is unique about this ethnic group in terms of how they see their community and its needs. Other groups, based on their unique history and social relations with the dominant group will come up with a different set of relevant research topics. Because one can learn a lot about an ethnic group by asking its members about legitimate areas of research, it is a very important question to ask for information purposes.

From these topics of interest to Japanese Americans, one can surmise that they have had problems with drug abuse, especially among the Sansei during the 1970s. They are losing their ethnic identification as they become more

Americanized with each generation and are concerned about this. They are aware of mental health problems such as depression and anxiety (this could relate to ulcers) as well as marriage and family conflicts, and they see the need for counseling services. However, seeking help may be more problematic since there is still a stigma to getting counseling. They are worried about caregiving for the older generation, because many Japanese American women work full time and would not be able to provide adequate care to the frail seniors in their family. Many of the Sansei generation have married outside their ethnic group, so there is a concern about the impact this would have on the community and on families. Many Japanese Americans have moved away from an ethnic community, so there is some concern about changes in residential patterns. Where do the Japanese Americans go when they get married or find a job? What happens to the extended family network with residential mobility? These are questions that a sociologist could research and help them answer.

Concern for the health and well-being of a community can also be seen in the topics of spousal battering and child abuse. Domestic violence is high in Asian communities so it is not surprising to see it here as a research concern. Lastly, they are interested in the Yonsei or fourth generation, just as the author was earlier in this chapter. How viable of a group will the Yonsei be ethnically with the high rate of out-marriage and assimilation taking place among Japanese Americans? Will they be able to preserve the culture and legacy of the Japanese American community?

Because Japanese Americans have been labeled a model minority, their mental health problems, violence toward women and older adults, and inadequate caregiving resources for the elderly will go unnoticed by the larger society (Weaver 2005, 174–75). Yet, the ethnic group will notice these problems and their voice becomes important in alerting the public to what is really the issue. Their concerns are all good research topics if anyone wants to study them.

## When Research becomes a Nuisance

Respondents considered research a nuisance when the same people are interviewed repeatedly or when they just don't have the time to be interviewed. Some respondents have been interviewed a number of times by the same type of researcher, that is, a college student doing a Japanese American cultural or community study. This student will be writing a paper and will ask for figures that the respondent has already given over and over again to other students. This can be a nuisance. Yet, there are other individuals who would be willing to be interviewed anytime and have all the patience in the world.

For some Japanese Americans and Japanese, the type of questions asked can be a nuisance. For example, if the questions have to do with such sensitive topics as sex, finances, and deviant behavior, the respondents are reluctant to answer them. In cases where respondents are very traditional, they may be unwilling to reveal anything negative about themselves or the community, because they are very conscious of how others regard them. If pressed to answer, they would be evasive or change the subject. According to respondents, the traditional Japanese American usually will be very polite in order to please the interviewer and will not display any anger or signs of irritation even when he is being asked bothersome questions.

Like other ethnic groups, repetitious interviewing can be a nuisance for many Japanese Americans. They are also aware of topics that would be sensitive for them such as sex, finances, and deviant behavior. The deviant behavior would be especially negative to this group because it is shameful to the family, so respondents are likely to keep it a secret not only from the community but from the researcher as well. Japanese Americans will tend to be accommodating to researchers but will not reveal things they consider private. However, if the researcher is Japanese American, respondents are likely to reveal more information because they trust the insider more than the outsider. This is also consistent with their clique behavior.

## Participation in Research

Japanese Americans would want to be informed about research that concerns their community. Possible avenues of informing the public would be through local Japanese newspapers such as *Kashu Mainichi* or *Rafu Shimpo*, through letters or by word of mouth. They would want to know the purpose of the research and what the study is on. A number of people would like to know the results of the research, which could be printed in the above newspapers or kept on file in the library of the Japanese American Cultural Center or the office of the Japanese American Citizen's League.

Some respondents would be more willing to participate in research studies if they were better informed about them or knew how the research results would create any changes in the community. They would like to know if something will come of their efforts since they put in valuable time to participate in the research. Other individuals would not be willing to participate as a respondent but would attend seminars about the research project or even write papers for it.

Believing strongly in research for educational purposes, Japanese Americans would not like research just thrust on them. They are curious and interested in serious research especially as it affects their community, and their involvement in research would depend on how knowledgeable they are about it. Japanese Americans are a very social group, and they would participate in activities at the community level if they felt they were a good cause.

## When Research is Offensive

A number of things were mentioned by respondents as being offensive to them or to community members. The following list describes these offenses.

1. With the older, traditional Japanese American, there is an emphasis placed on courtesy and politeness within the home, so the researcher should be careful not to violate these values by refusing any tea or food offered by the host or by being too direct or indifferent to them as human beings.
2. Japanese Americans do not like to be treated as subjects.
3. Some Japanese Americans would be very offended if confidential information about them was published so that their friends and neighbors would see it. They see the community as a "small world" where everyone knows about everyone else, and should anything negative about them be made public, they would lose face in the community.
4. Other community members would object to the researcher's style of interviewing and behavior. For example, an overly persistent person or a person who continues with the research when the respondent is tired of answering would not be appreciated. Humility is valued, so that an assertive or overly demanding person would be offensive to them.
5. Another offensive behavior would be to misperceive the person's degree of ethnicity like when someone mistakes a Japanese American for a recently arrived Japanese immigrant. This can happen when the researcher or other person remarks on how well the respondent speaks English, which may be the only language he or she knows.
6. Some Japanese Americans would be displeased if the research is vaguely stated and difficult to understand. They would want clear instructions about it and a statement of a legitimate research purpose.
7. Other respondents would be very concerned about the accuracy of research conclusions, especially if data collection was hasty and scanty. They would be concerned about false information being published about them.

From these responses, one can see some cultural imperatives being stressed, especially for the sake of the older generation of Japanese Americans and those who are more traditional. Visitors to the home of a Japanese family should maintain politeness and reserve by accepting the tea or food that is offered to them. Graciously accepting the hospitality of the host and hostess also means getting engaged in sociable conversation rather than going directly into business matters of the research agenda. If the researcher goes straight into the interview, Japanese Americans would feel like they are being treated as subjects and this would offend them. Politeness is important when interviewing Japanese American respondents who use nonverbal cues to let others know how they are feeling. They would want the researcher to know when to stop asking questions because the respondents may be getting tired or may not want to answer certain questions. Persistence, or being overdemanding with questions, is considered rude.

The issue of shame also comes up again here where some Japanese Americans would not want negative information about them publicized, or they would be embarrassed. Related to this is their concern that the research purpose is legitimate and the results are accurate. They would be embarrassed if they got involved in something that discredited them.

A final note can be made about how respondents are addressed by researchers. One should never assume that just because a respondent is older and has a Japanese first and last name that he or she is from Japan. There are many older Nisei in their 60s and 70s who speak only English and are very Americanized. They are to be distinguished from individuals who are from Japan that may speak English well, but usually with an accent. There are also some older Japanese Americans who were born in the United States but raised in Japan, and they never learned to speak English very well when they came back to the United States because they did not have to interact that much with the American public. They would be called Kibei and would not consider themselves to be similar to the Japanese from Japan.

## Preferred Behavior around Community Members

According to respondents, Japanese Americans mainly stress the need for politeness by the researcher no matter what segment of the population he/she is addressing. They don't like to be treated as minorities who are spoken to in a condescending way, which can occur very easily when the interviewer speaks to them as though they don't understand what is being said.

Many of the first generation Japanese may not speak English; therefore, it would be advisable to use an interpreter in this case or become familiar with the Japanese language. If one is interviewing an elderly person, there should be more consideration for the speed of the interview. It might be necessary to go slower and to wait at greater length for responses.

One should make a special effort to observe any formal rituals that the family members are displaying and accommodate one's self to them as much as possible, for example, tea drinking and removing one's shoes before entering the home. Restraint and formality is appreciated by some individuals, while friendliness is valued by others. Among the elderly or traditional Japanese Americans, restraint and politeness are especially important.

It is a good idea to approach respondents through a contact person who may be a friend of the respondent or an influential community member. The contact person is one who would endorse the project and assume the responsibility for any negative consequences of the research. He/she would also help to ease the relationship between strangers during an interview session. It would be to the advantage of the researcher to have some knowledge of the background, history, and culture of Japanese Americans before going out into the field.

As mentioned earlier, Japanese Americans do not like to be treated as subjects who are spoken to but not interacted with in a sociable way. This would be reinforcing their minority status rather than treating them as equals. If a researcher were to mistake a respondent for someone who is from Japan rather than a Japanese American, then he could be offensive by speaking very slowly or carefully, as though this person didn't know English very well. This is why it is important to be sociable first and find out who is Issei and, therefore, less likely to know English fluently and be more assimilated. If an individual does not speak or understand English well, a family member is the most likely person to be a translator unless the researcher is bilingual and can speak Japanese.

Trust is a major issue for Japanese Americans when they are dealing with outsiders. One can see this in the responses above indicating that Japanese Americans want a contact person who knows the respondents and can vouch for the validity of the research project and the credibility of the researcher. It is not because of cultural differences that they need a contact person, as the Westerner will find Japanese Americans to be quite assimilated in general. It is more likely to be a result of experiencing anti-Japanese prejudice and discrimination before, during, and after World War II. During World War II, Japanese Americans were treated as subjects with no rights when they were in the relocation centers, and they continued to experience patronizing behavior from others during this entire anti-Japanese period. It is not surprising, then, that respondents want the researcher to know about them, their history and culture, and what they have gone through as American citizens.

## Behavioral Patterns and Aspects of Japanese American Character

Based on these findings on Japanese Americans from the Pilot Ethnic Research Training Project, one can conclude that, as a group, these individuals are sometimes very reticent about giving out information to a researcher. Perhaps they feel it may reflect negatively on them, or they feel uneasy about giving information directly. The researcher should avoid being too persistent or probing for answers when the people are holding back on responses. Sometimes the Japanese American respondent will open up and speak very freely when proper protocol has been observed, such as socializing and chatting before the interview. Japanese respondents who are traditional expect this socializing before the interviewing begins.

Japanese Americans can sometimes be very subtle in mannerisms, which give them the impression of being nonverbal (Kitano, 1969); however, this does not mean they are quiet. This nonverbalness is more often displayed around a researcher who is not Japanese American, because Japanese Americans may feel uncomfortable saying things to an outsider. Some of these individuals may be less verbal than others because they may not be socially active in the community. However, the people in general are community-centered and feel a strong sense of identification with each other as a group (Miyamoto 1939). Toward each other there is also a sense of obligation to help one another and to express gratitude for favors done or services rendered. There is especially a strong obligation to serve older adults, and these elderly are highly respected by the community and treated with deference by those younger (Montero 1980).

As a rule, Japanese Americans do not display extreme forms of behavior such as loudness, aggressiveness, and excessive talking or speaking about themselves. These behaviors would appear boastful and Japanese Americans do not like to call attention to themselves. Culturally, they tend to use an indirect approach to questioning and answering each other, which may not result in complete or specific answers in an interview situation. Many of them may skirt around a subject rather than respond to it directly or may not be willing to speak about personal things directly. This is a circular way of talking that reflects Japanese American politeness (Lyman 1970, 85). A researcher who learns how to interview respondents in an indirect way would get good results from Japanese Americans.

There are some Nisei or Issei (women more so than men) who may be afraid to be interviewed and will refuse the first or second time they are asked. They may have never been interviewed before and will be hesitant to offer any information. This may reflect shyness, or it may indicate a pattern of traditional social structure where the male enacts the more dominant role within the family. The wife will defer to him and expect him to be the one who answers the questions. This pattern is more prevalent among older Japanese Americans. The researcher may be able to persuade these individuals to be researched if he uses discretion in manners and approach.

## CONCLUSIONS

Japanese Americans are an interesting group to understand. Though they stand out physically like other Asian Americans and look very ethnic, they are quite assimilated into American culture. Yet, this assimilation is neither complete nor similar to other ethnic groups, simply because Japanese Americans have had a unique history here and still maintain in subtle ways the cultural heritage of their ancestors. Coming to the United States early, they have followed the trail of Chinese immigrants to the West Coast and became the second major Asian group to enter the United States. This early immigration history would result in rapid cultural assimilation for the Japanese, but the relocation experience during World War II made the group insular and even more community-focused than before.

Though friendly and sociable as a group, they are complex underneath. By culture, they have been taught to be polite and respectful toward others, yet by historical circumstances they have been taught to be wary and suspicious of outsiders. The outsider is usually a non-Japanese person, but when it comes to clique membership, the outsider is anyone who does not have the proper introduction to join the group.

As pointed out earlier, clique formation is alive and well even among the Sansei, who supposedly are very Americanized and have a high rate of intermarriage. The insular nature of a clique would imply that it provides safety and security to individuals who have experienced a hostile society. Though discrimination and prejudice toward Japanese Americans have weakened significantly since World War II, cliques may serve to protect ethnic members from those they do not trust, as well as reinforce ethnic identity through social ties.

For the researcher studying this population, it is important to know about cliques and how they operate. In a cultural sense, it is not unusual for the Japanese people to use a social contact when they want to meet someone. It is proper etiquette and formal, and this is how arranged marriages in Japan are conducted. For example, a person called a "go between" will initiate the contact between families that have prospective candidates for marriage. Once proper introductions are made, it then becomes appropriate to begin the socializing process. Respondents have mentioned the need for the researcher to introduce his research and himself properly to the community, and a contact person would really facilitate this process. Considering all the anti-Japanese sentiment experienced earlier by the Japanese, and being treated as a minority group with few rights, it is not surprising that cliques would be maintained today by younger generations of Japanese Americans, and that Japanese Americans would require evidence of trustworthiness from a researcher.

This interaction pattern fits the interdependence idea and the need to affiliate suggested by Weaver (2005) that is common to other Asian American groups as well. As assimilation proceeds with new cohorts of Chinese, Korean, Japanese, and Filipino immigrants coming to the United States, it is likely that the Asian American community will maintain itself because of this cultural value of networking with others that are similar to one's own group.

# Chapter 9

# Mexican Americans

## LATINO POPULATIONS

Known as the fastest growing ethnic population in the United States, Latino populations are grouped together and also called Hispanics, but their diversity is more evident than their similarities. Their common linkage is their historical tie to Spain's language and values, but they are found around the globe wherever Spaniards have colonized and settled to create the mixed racial groups of people called Latinos (Weaver 2005, 139). Most Latino populations are concentrated in the West and in urban areas, and their diversity encompasses national origins from all the South American and Central American nations, some of the Caribbean nations, Spain, and Mexico. In California, this diversity can be seen by individuals identifying themselves as Ecuadorians, Salvadorans, Puerto Ricans, Nicaraguans, Peruvians, Dominicans, Argentineans, and Mexicans. Their voices are easily heard in Southern California as they show pride in national origin and in the unique cultural blends they have brought over.

The author has seen the cultural diversity among Latino populations through her travels, especially in food and language variations. Though Spanish is the language spoken in Latino countries, its variation is noticeable from one country to another. Southern Californians are more familiar with the Spanish spoken in Mexico, which makes the Spanish in Costa Rica easier to follow than the Spanish in Spain or Cuba. The food variations reflect climate and environmental influences so that different ingredients are used and different dishes are prepared. The cultural diversity extends to different celebrations, different religious rituals, clothing styles, and artifacts. However, similarities may exist in terms of close-knit family ties, clear-cut gender roles for men and women, and the value placed on religion (Ibid., 145–47).

Latino populations will also show diversity in their immigration history and status, their socioeconomic status, and their level of assimilation. Each Latino population must be studied more in-depth in order to understand the true nature of their ethnic experience here. However, this is beyond the scope of this book. What is evident is that Latino populations have been treated differently in terms of immigration rights, and this has affected their status here (legal and illegal), their socioeconomic level, and their family life.

Today we are seeing more transnational families and mothers than ever before. This is where fathers or mothers work in the United States while their children live in the Latino nation of origin. We are also seeing more bi-national families that consist of undocumented immigrants and their children who are U.S. citizens through birth or legal residents (Taylor 2002, 90). These family patterns can create unique problems for Latino populations, though it can also provide them with more flexible ways of adapting.

As a therapist, the author knows of Latino families where children have been left with grandparents or other relatives in the parent's country of origin while the parents stay in the United States to work. The children are parented by other family members and raised in another culture. However, once the parents save up enough money to bring the children to the United States, the children are much older and quite estranged from the parents they have not seen for years. This can create bonding problems between parents and children, rebellion on the part of the children to parental authority, inconsistent or harsh discipline on the part of the parents, and generational conflict. The situation is compounded when the newly reunited children have to adjust to new siblings that were born in their absence.

Immigration issues affect Latino populations in different ways, but it is the Mexican population that is particularly concerned about new immigration laws as they are at the center of much controversy about immigration in the border states with Mexico. The rest of this chapter will be devoted to this large and significant minority population that has been studied as part of the Pilot Ethnic Research Training Program.

## MEXICAN AMERICANS

### Immigration and History

As the largest segment of the Latino population in the United States, Mexican Americans and Mexican-origin immigrants are creating an ethnic group that is diverse, very urban, and constantly increasing in numbers. Yet, the native-born Mexican population is increasing today at a much slower rate than the number of foreign-born Mexicans (Taylor 2002, 81), and this is creating some interesting dynamics in our society with both positive and negative consequences. On the one hand, it is easy for the American population to be economically impacted by foreign-born Mexicans that have come here both legally and illegally for employment. These immigrants make major contributions to the American economy by working in so many industries; but at the same time, they are considered competitors for working-class jobs that others want. On the other hand, the visibility of this group makes it more difficult to see who the Mexican Americans are, as they have integrated into American society through upward mobility over several generations. However, the negative stereotypes the American public has of Mexican immigrants could easily be placed on this group as well because the two groups are lumped together in the public mind.

Of interest to the author is how the immigrant group from Mexico and Mexican Americans relate to each other given recent efforts to seal the Mexican/U.S. border and cut down on illegal immigration. At one point, many Mexican Americans had an immigration history in their families and they probably experienced the same type of prejudice and discrimination that current immigrants are receiving. Many Mexican Americans continue to experience prejudice and discrimination, so their ability to trust the dominant group would be questionable and one can hypothesize that they would have a close connection with Mexican immigrants. The Immigration Rights Movement going on in Los Angeles, which was highlighted by a massive peaceful demonstration in Los Angeles on May 1, 2006, may be an indication that the immigrant group can get support not only from Mexican Americans but others in society as well.

The two groups have also come to American society to improve their economic situation and they have labored in various industries both urban and rural. Though many Mexican Americans have become middle class today, there are many who are working class as well, and family members from both groups can travel back and forth to Mexico preserving language and family culture. Instead of seeing these two groups as really separate, an "alternation theory" would say that the more recent group of immigrants would quickly learn two languages, have two cultures, and be able to see the world through two different value lenses simply because it is composed of transnational families who work and live in one country, but connect with and support a family in another country (Falicov 2005, 230). By adapting quickly to American society, while retaining their Mexican culture, this group is likely to be absorbed into the native Mexican American population, which would create a tie between them that would not only be through cultural heritage but also through history in the United States.

Mexican Americans have had a long history in the United States as an oppressed minority group. Having had ownership of land in California and the Southwest before the war between Mexico and the United States (1846–1848), Mexicans were a proud, dominant ethnic group living in Mexico's territories. However, Mexico's defeat in the war changed all that. Through various means, such as wholesale transfer of land from Mexican to Anglo ownership, or through robbery, intimidation, fraud, or heavy litigation costs to defend land holdings, Mexican families lost their land to the majority group (Estrada et al. 1995). Through this early experience of losing their land and their dominance in California and the Southwest, Mexicans who became American citizens by default had good reason to not trust Anglo Americans. Added to this injury is the ongoing insult of being perceived and treated as a low-status labor force, which carries its own consequences of prejudice and discrimination.

Mexican immigrants have been coming to the United States for years to work in the labor force. During the Depression when jobs were scarce, Mexicans were especially seen as a threat to America's economy and job market. Since many of them were unemployed and applying for public relief, they became an easy target for deportation under "voluntary repatriation," which was really a way to get them off the relief rolls despite having American citizenship (Estrada 1995). Is this threat any different today? Have things changed that much since the Depression Era for Mexican Americans and Mexican immigrants?

The Immigration Rights Movement today is bringing into full public view the hardships and oppression of this large minority group. For years Mexican Americans have been victims of deportation under false charges. Mexican immigrants and citizens have been blamed for taking away jobs from the working-class Anglo American by working for lower wages. Yet isn't this what capitalism is all about? Our nation was built on the substandard wages of exploited immigrant workers from Europe who are now part of the majority group. Of course, these workers were abused and impoverished, too, and did go through unemployment during the Great Depression. However, they did not become targets of discrimination and prejudice like the Mexican immigrant population because they did not stand out as a distinct ethnic group of color.

Today, a young Mexican American woman can go into a department store and be followed around by a sales attendant. She may have money in her purse and a middle-class background, but she will be scrutinized more carefully for possible shoplifting than a Caucasian or Japanese American woman. A young Mexican American male could hang out with other Mexican American friends and be perceived as a gang member. A Mexican American man or woman of dark complexion could be viewed as an illegal immigrant, even though they have a high education and a good income. All of these possibilities would increase the likelihood that Mexican Americans would not trust the dominant group, just as the dominant group distrusts the Mexican Americans they perceive in a negative way.

Based on the general stereotyping of Mexicans and Mexican Americans in negative ways without the public separating the two groups, it is easy to see how both groups may align with each other when it comes to certain basic rights. However, it does not mean that all Mexican Americans would sympathize and identify with Mexican immigrants. Those who are more assimilated may not support the Immigration Rights Movement due to differences in political, economic, and cultural views. Mexican Americans may also not want to affiliate with Mexican immigrants if they look down on this group and consider themselves superior to them. Other ethnic groups like Japanese Americans do consider themselves a separate group from the Japanese from Japan who are seen as foreign even though they have a similar ancestry. It is the different histories of the two Japanese groups that make them less likely to identify with each other. This would not be the case with Mexican Americans and Mexican immigrants who are much closer to their ancestral land compared to other ethnic groups and share the pride of a strong Hispanic culture in the Southwest. These two groups are more likely than other groups to support immigrants especially when their own relatives may be coming over to join them in the United States.

Mexican Americans stand out from the majority group in other ways besides skin color and culture. In general, they are a population with a young median age and high fertility. They have a low median income, a low high school completion rate, and a concentration of family members in blue collar jobs (Mindel, Habenstein, and Wright Jr. 1998). This would indicate a high poverty rate with this group and difficulty moving up the socioeconomic ladder since high school and college completion is a necessity for higher paying jobs. When Mexican Americans are perceived as having a low education and a high dropout rate from schools by teachers and school counselors, they may not be given the best education and encouragement. Many of them do not pursue a higher degree because they are not given the assistance to get that far. This, in turn, could affect their grades and attendance and create a self-fulfilling prophecy. From here, it is easy to see why the low socioeconomic status of Mexican Americans perpetuates itself. Unable to get good paying jobs because of low education and discrimination in hiring, Mexican American youth could join the ranks of the unemployed, or end up in prison, or work in dead-end jobs. Frustration and lack of trust of the majority group is a consequence of unequal opportunities and rights.

## The Importance of Culture

Mexican Americans have preserved many aspects of their culture in the Southwest and California because these areas were originally Mexico's territories. Their language predominates in California and the Southwest because it is spoken in the homes of many Mexican Americans and reinforced in the community. With the influx of immigrant children from Mexico and other Spanish-speaking nations, being bilingual is one of the preferred criteria in the hiring of teachers. It is also an important, preferred criterion in the hiring of employees in many service occupations from medicine to counseling, and in many other jobs where Hispanic individuals are a majority of the customers. This preferred criterion in hiring is encouraging more people to learn Spanish in order to acquire better paying jobs. It is also resulting in the hiring of many individuals of Hispanic origin, which will eventually lead to the upward mobility of these groups that include Mexican Americans from working-class backgrounds. As more bilingual individuals are hired into jobs that serve the Mexican population, the Spanish-speaking Mexicans will receive better services throughout the larger society.

These are positive results of the Spanish language's dominance in Southern California and other areas. Spanish can be learned in schools and in college where it is easily available to non-Spanish speaking populations. One can learn Spanish from friends, neighbors, employees, or by going to Mexico on a frequent basis. However, there is a downside to the predominance of Spanish in our nation.

There can be strong disapproval of Spanish being spoken in public by individuals who dislike anything foreign being displayed in our society. These individuals may also dislike any ethnic language that is spoken outside of the home whether it is Chinese, a Filipino dialect, or Vietnamese. During the early 1900s when many immigrants were coming from Europe for employment, this same dislike of foreigners was impacting society, only on a much larger scale. It resulted in major acts of discrimination and strong waves of prejudice and racism toward immigrant groups. For Mexican Americans who are already being stereotyped in a negative way as low-income workers and illegal immigrants, the visibility of their culture through language could also result in discrimination in education, hiring, and community services. The end result of these forms of negative treatment would be a desire for Mexican Americans to turn inward to family and their ethnic community where it is safe to trust others.

The family has always been important in Mexican culture. Whether the family is more traditional or modern, extended or nuclear in form, the Mexican family maintains itself through a high fertility rate and lower divorce rate than other ethnic groups. A family orientation continues even when assimilation takes place because the extended kinship ties are still important and the family maintains a stable, cohesive structure where members know their place, receive support, and feel a sense of belonging (Mindel et al. 1998, 161). This strong sense of family is reinforced by the value of "personalismo" or an interpersonal relationship that is close and person-centered rather than object-centered or concerned with individual achievements. Bean, Perry, and Bedell (2001) mention that in a counseling session, one can achieve this "personalismo" with Hispanic clients by interacting with them in a warm and genuine way and showing an interest in the individual by asking about hobbies, music, and family. By doing so, the therapist not only gains the client's trust but also his/her cooperation in the therapy process.

On a more personal note, the author can relate to this "personalismo" by remembering visits to the homes of childhood friends who were Mexican American. It was the mother and grandmother, especially, who treated guests with genuine courtesy, hospitality, generosity, and respect. For example, if the girlfriend was eating a popsicle and did not offer the visitor one, she was scolded by her grandmother and told to get the guest a popsicle. Food was always generously offered even though these working-class families with several children and only one income did not have that much money. The author would spend the night with one girlfriend who lived down the street from her, and her mother was caring and considerate and made her feel very welcome in their home. When the author's father passed away when she was a teenager, this mother called her up to offer her sympathy and cried with her. Her way of being person-centered was appreciated by the author.

Another example comes to mind for the author of Mexican American hospitality and courtesy. She remembers going to a party with her sister and the sister's Mexican American boyfriend when she was a teenager. The party was at the home of one of his relatives. When they were received at the door, the author was surprised to see a large, extended network of people waiting inside the door to greet them formally by shaking their hand. The author greeted the grandmother first and then all the family members down to the teenagers and children. She was surprised to see the teenagers just as polite and courteous as the grown-ups. On the street by themselves, these teenagers may be perceived by others as gang members, but here in this setting they were part of the extended family and observant of the cultural value of "personalismo."

The strong, family-oriented values of Mexican Americans also make them come to the defense of each other when threatened by others. The author's girlfriend was taught by her family to defend cousins, nieces, and sisters who were attacked or insulted by nonfamily members. She was ready to gang up on these individuals with other family members of the same age group in order to fight back. In a way, this seemed like a form of machismo displayed by the oldest child in the family in an effort to protect and defend family members who were treated unfairly.

Culturally, such values as "machismo" and "personalismo" not only strengthen family members' ties to one another, but they also inform the family of who is not to be trusted. When Mexican Americans are not treated with courtesy, respect, friendliness, hospitality, consideration, and concern for who they are as people, they will not be able to trust that their needs will be met. With family members and others of their same ethnic group, they may be able to predict behaviors that are congruent with these cultural beliefs. However, when they encounter outsiders who may judge them according to stereotypes or who discriminate against them, they are more likely to stay away from these individuals and not cooperate with them.

Mexican Americans have been studied by researchers for a long time, and similar to African Americans, researchers have focused on them as a lower-income minority group. This has reinforced the stereotypes of Mexican Americans as being a subordinate group in our society rather than highlighting their diversity, accomplishments, and contributions to American society. Little research has been done on middle-class and upper-class Mexican Americans and their cultural retention, ethnic identity, and out-marriage rate with its consequences. This information is needed in order to have a more integrated perspective of this ethnic group.

## Data from the Pilot Ethnic Research Training Project

Responses from twenty-two Mexican Americans were collected in 1980 through in-depth interviews, and these responses can be analyzed in terms of how the ethnic group is today. As mentioned in chapter 1, the responses are from both community members and agency directors, and they reflect a time period when ethnic sentiments were quite strong.

## Attitude toward the University

There were many Mexican American respondents who viewed the university as being out of reach for their community members. Individuals may know it exists, but it is not realistic for them to attend since they must work to survive in this society. The university is for those who can afford to go. Parents may not encourage their children to go on to higher education if it is unrealistic economically. For these individuals, though, the university is viewed with respect, and younger people are more likely to know about the university than older people.

For other individuals, the university is viewed with apprehension and irritation because it is unresponsive to their needs or it reflects "Establishment" ways. Some might categorize it with the government and census work of which they are frightened. Lastly, a number of people are simply ignorant of the university and are not aware of what and where it is.

These comments would definitely reflect the attitudes of lower-income Mexican Americans and recent immigrants from Mexico. The university would not be affordable for many children of immigrant parents, though by the time these children are college age, they may be attending the university through financial aid. California State University–Dominguez Hills graduates many students of Hispanic background, and many times these students are the first ones in their families to receive a BA degree.

## Attitude toward Researchers

For many Mexican Americans, researchers would be welcome in their community if their studies benefit the people, and in some cases, research is considered necessary to effect change. It is viewed as a good way to open up communication between the campus and community and might encourage more Mexican Americans to go to college.

For other respondents, researchers would not be welcome because they are seen as prying, busybodies, or elitist types. Some individuals pointed out that there are community members who fear data collection because it is threatening to them and may mean that someone is checking up on them, namely, government officials. The issue of trust is a major one for the more traditional and older Mexican American with less education compared to those who are more assimilated. They may not trust the researcher and research because they don't know much about the university. For others who are concerned about deportation and its effect in their community, researchers would be especially threatening. These respondents would not be receptive to research questions because they do not trust what the data may be used for even though it is collected by students or professors.

On the other hand, the very fact that researchers from the university are present in the Mexican American community might result in a public relations effect. As they spread the word about who they are and what they are trying to do for educational purposes, it might attract enough positive attention that people would get interested in the university.

## Legitimate Areas of Research

Education was mentioned most often by these respondents as an area needing research. Other topics that should be researched are community-university relations, educational opportunities, elementary reading programs, high school dropouts, and the teaching of a positive self-image among Mexican American youth. Other areas of equal importance are the economic needs of the community, job opportunities, medical and mental health needs, and research on senior citizens.

Most individuals felt that research is never a nuisance as long as it is well-prepared and responsive to the needs of the community. When research does cover topics like those mentioned by respondents, cooperation is more likely. Yet, for some individuals, repetitious questioning would be unwelcome if the questions did not deal with what the community would consider survival problems. Questionnaires and studies that are long-term and do not end quickly can be a nuisance to individuals who are busy or uninterested in the study.

In addition, community members may not want to be asked questions on personal topics. These are not legitimate areas to cover, especially when the researcher is not welcome in the first place because he is a stranger. Yet, other people will show politeness and friendliness and appear to be comfortable answering questions, so the researcher will not know for sure if he is a nuisance to them. It is preferable that the researcher not take advantage of their hospitality by coming back a number of times to ask questions. If he wants to research a family, it should be done all in one shot rather than a number of times.

Like other ethnic groups covered in this book, Mexican Americans are concerned about economic problems and the need for community services. Educational opportunities and services are important because there is a high dropout rate with Mexican American high school students. Educational encouragement for youth from grades K–12 would keep them from turning to drugs and gangs and help them believe in themselves as achievers rather than become school failures. Starting at the younger ages with reading programs and tutoring would help students adjust to the educational system more readily. In today's schools, with their emphasis on bilingual teachers and staff, the language problem would not be as critical. However, having adequate resources at schools in Mexican American neighborhoods is crucial. Fortunately, schools in the Los Angeles area do come equipped with computers and offer medical services and mental health counseling for both the student and his/her family.

## Participation in Research

Before participating in research, respondents would first like to be informed about the project through various ways such as the media, newsletters, verbal communication, announcements (through an agency or public meetings), formal publications, or through church. A number of respondents stated their willingness to participate, and one respondent felt that young people could also get involved in research if it were publicized in the right places. Sometimes an individual wanted to participate in research because of an interest he/she had in a specific topic. For example, one person mentioned high school research as an area of interest, while another person mentioned research on small children. The majority of respondents felt that once the research was completed, it was important to share research results with the community.

Advertising a research project in the Mexican American community seems to be an important way to get people involved. There are many ways that one can find out about the research because people are actively involved in their community and interact with each other. The research just needs to be posted in public places or announced in places like church where the attendance of community members is high. It also appears that family members of all ages could participate in research. Mexican Americans do get involved as a family in many different types of activities.

## Things That Offend the People

There are many things that would offend Mexican Americans when researchers approach them. These would include the following things: ignoring the needs of the community, acting in a condescending way, being disrespectful, having preconceived notions about the people or being judgmental, lacking awareness of customs and cultural differences, expressing superiority, being pushy, and displaying pity toward the people.

Respondents felt that questions should be asked in a polite way using the right tone of voice, and no racial overtones should be implied while communicating. They further pointed out that Mexican Americans would be offended by the researcher showing a lack of knowledge about their group so that he ends up reiterating stereotypes that are negative to the people.

These responses from Mexican Americans relate to the cultural materials presented earlier. Because they believe in treating guests with respect, hospitality, and a personal concern for the individual, they would also like to be treated this way by strangers. If the researcher is aware of these aspects of their culture, then he would be treating them according to their expectations. It sounds like Mexican Americans, too often, are not treated politely or in a personable way because people do not know their ways and thus behave toward them according to stereotypes about the group or treating them in a patronizing way.

## Behavior around Community Members

In general, respondents felt that researchers should show sensitivity, humility, consideration, and cordiality in their behavior around Mexican Americans and treat people with respect. Openness and amiability are desirable because the people like friendliness more than solemnity. Showing respect for the culture of the people, dealing honestly with community members, showing genuine interest in them, and being natural were other things of importance to Mexican Americans. One way to show respect for the culture is to speak the native language to the elderly who are less likely to know English. This is desirable even if the person does not speak Spanish that well.

With younger people, the researcher should attempt to speak their type of language and be aware of their way of seeing things. With older persons, there may be a need for more socializing and getting acquainted because these individuals may be more suspicious of the stranger. In traditional families, it might be appropriate to address the male first or the husband. When asking people questions, they should be appropriate to the social group one is addressing. For example, younger people could be asked questions about school; however, the elderly might be more interested in questions dealing with health care, social security, and housing.

When first meeting people from the community, respondents felt that the researcher should properly introduce himself. In some cases formality is expected, as with older Mexican Americans and those more traditional, and the researcher should display reserve and social distance toward them. Forwardness is a sign of impertinence and rudeness to these individuals. With other community members who have been here longer and who are less traditional, informality might be preferred; however, this does not mean familiarity or the use of Anglo clichés of the Spanish language such as, "vaya con dios."

It is proper to shake hands with everyone present when first greeting a family. The man of the house should be greeted first and then his wife and children. When explaining the research purpose, the researcher should be natural and sincere and introduce the research carefully. The term "study" rather than "research" should be used, because the latter may be construed as an experiment which people dislike (they are familiar with research on monkeys). Stating the goals of the research is important, because the people would want to know how the study will help their community. They will be more cooperative if they know the research will benefit them in some way. Information should be shared in a two-way conversation during the interview, and it should be warm and friendly rather than stiff.

Respondents mentioned a few other things of which the researcher should be aware. One of these is eye contact, which should be focused on the individual speaking but not so directly that one is staring at him/her too intensely. This is a sign of directness again which is rude. If food or any beverages are offered, they should be graciously accepted. If for any reason the appointment must be cancelled, let the respondent know.

Again the emphasis on "personalismo" is evident in these responses from Mexican Americans. The way one approaches family members is very important in first impressions. If a person is friendly, sociable, respectful and person-oriented, the guest will make a good impression on the family. This would imply that you are interested in who these people are and this would include their culture and family. That is why it is appropriate to converse with family members according to their age and their traditions. If one tries to converse with an older, traditional grandmother who does not speak English, it does not matter if one's Spanish is quite bad. The very fact that you are attempting to communicate with someone this old and respected in her own language shows that you are person-centered.

Mexican Americans are very conscious of the correct way to interact with people in their culture, because they are experts at socializing intergenerationally. They are used to being around extended family members and friends of all ages for many different social occasions such as weddings, family parties, church and holiday events, and quinccaneras. Of course, other ethnic groups can also spend a great deal of time with extended family members and friends on many social occasions, but they will follow the norms of their culture in terms of proper interaction.

As mentioned earlier by the author, shaking hands with everyone present when first greeting a family is a norm in Mexican American culture. Beginning with the person who has the highest status in the family, it is important to shake hands with each individual, including children. Good eye contact is important, because it expresses an interest in the person one is talking to. Accepting food and beverages from the hostess when they are offered gives the guest a chance to express gratitude for the hospitality he/she is receiving.

Once the formalities are over and rapport has been built through polite socializing, it would be proper to explain the research purpose. Using language that is familiar and clear to the people is important. It is also important to show

how the research is significant to these individuals or beneficial to the community. Allowing for lots of discussion by family members of the research idea would get them more interested in participating in the project as a family. Mexican Americans are very family oriented and they are likely to get involved in research as a family or community if this research is beneficial to them.

## Cultural Beliefs and Taboos

Respondents mentioned certain topics that are taboo to discuss mainly because of religious beliefs. They include sex, abortion, personal family matters, and church issues. It is possible that with a proper introduction by a respected community person, some individuals such as seniors might be willing to answer questions on taboo subjects, but husbands and wives should be interviewed separately on personal matters. Other taboo areas are marital relations, family size, income (sometimes), and medical information about women such as pregnancies, hysterectomies, and even tuberculosis. The latter can be a reason for social ostracization, and some women are shameful of disclosing it.

In general, personal questions are usually not welcome because they violate one's privacy. Though Mexican Americans are friendly and gracious, they do not reveal their personal life to strangers and do not like close physical contact. Hand shaking is fine, but not hugging and kissing.

The people have strong family ties in most cases, and they are very proud of their family and culture. Within the family there is a hierarchy of statuses, and the researcher would do well to address the head of the household first. It is likely to be a male and sometimes an elder. In traditional families a female will not even open the door to a male stranger. If he requests an interview with her, the wife must wait until her husband comes home before she will talk to the interviewer and in her husband's presence.

Language is very important to the people, and they are pleased when the researcher has made an attempt to learn it before interviewing those in the community who are more traditional. It is also to the researcher's advantage if he understands the more subtle behavioral cues that the people display, such as being friendly even when they are displeased with the researcher. Because of strong values placed on hospitality and harmony, they will not disclose negative feelings or emotions. Hospitality is very important in the Mexican American culture. It will be graciously offered, and it should be well-received by the researcher. To show a lack of appreciation for the kindness of the host would be very offensive.

Mexican Americans can have strong traditions related to religion and health care. They may protect these beliefs by keeping them within the family, though one can find out about these beliefs through books that have been written on Mexican American folk beliefs related to healing and sickness and their use of curanderas and folk remedies (Martinez 1978; Clark 1970). Traditions do not change that easily when kept within an extended family network that receives reinforcement from the Mexican American community. Therefore, it is not surprising that respondents would mention taboo areas that they would be reluctant to discuss with a researcher. Some of these areas would be sensitive for other ethnic groups to discuss as well, such as medical information and personal family matters, so it may be that the degree of assimilation is important in how open respondents will be about these topics.

## SUMMARY

As the largest group within the Latino population, Mexican Americans have been influencing and impacting American society for centuries. As the fastest growing minority group in the nation, they are physically and culturally visible as a people, yet many times invisible in terms of basic human rights. Similar to other Latino populations in the United States in terms of language, strong family ties, and religion, they are also diverse in their degree of assimilation, socioeconomic level, and ethnic identification. However, their long history in the United States makes them distinct from other Latino populations.

Because of this diversity, which includes a large immigrant population from Mexico and a native Mexican American population in various stages of assimilation, this ethnic group faces challenges to its identity. Important family values can become less important to each generation here as Mexican American youth acculturate faster than their elders. Mexican American women may seek greater equality with males in the home because they are receiving it in the larger society. Intermarriages will accelerate the rate of assimilation as it does for other ethnic groups. What will become the means by which a Mexican American can develop a healthy ethnic identity that is not based on skin color alone? This is the question Martinez (1978) raises as he voices concern for Mexican Americans living in a bicultural world. Values that conflict with the larger society can make the transition difficult, and discrimination and prejudice can make it difficult to trust the world outside the ethnic community. Perhaps it will require the forging of a new ethnic identity that incorporates the best of both the Mexican American and immigrant cultures. This new ethnic identity, if it happens, would certainly offer other Latino populations an example of what can be achieved in successful social and cultural adaptation.

# Chapter 10

# Samoan Americans

## PACIFIC ISLANDERS

Included in this large grouping of people called the Pacific Islanders are the descendants of indigenous settlers of the many Pacific Islands strewn from east to west in a large area south of Hawaii. They would include people from the following islands: Hawaii, Guam and the Mariana Islands, Samoa, Tonga, Tahiti, Fiji, Papua New Guinea, and the Solomon Islands (Weaver 2005, 191). Some of these islands have been exposed to western influences through early colonization and later developed a specific relationship to the United States. For example, Hawaii became a state while American Samoa and Guam came under United States jurisdiction as territories. These three groups are the largest in population size of the Pacific Islanders, and they are the most familiar to Americans.

In Southern California, one can find the largest group of Samoans outside of Samoa residing in the South Bay area. Other Pacific Islanders, like the Guamanians, have been around the Long Beach area since the author was growing up there. Since California is the closest mainland state for Pacific Island migration, it is not surprising that these populations would settle there first and establish communities that others would join over the years.

It is the diversity of these island histories and cultures that give the people their identity. However, Hawaii has been populated by so many Americans as well as other nationalities, and visited by so many tourists, that one could say the indigenous identity has been in crisis for a long time. The Native Hawaiian Movement was a response to this crisis, though its cultural emphasis is far overshadowed by that blend of Hawaiian culture with other cultures we call a "melting pot." This has produced pidgin English among Japanese Hawaiians and their famous "spam musubi" (rice ball topped with a square of dried seaweed and a slice of spam), among other "melting pot" traits.

However, "old Hawaii," as it is known through its ancient chants, hulas, and ceremonies, still reverberates through the islands as well as the legends and stories of spirits that still roam the islands. Kauai is a great place to get a feel for this because it is still "Hawaiian" in its small towns, Hawaiian foods, and legends of the Menehune. The Menehune were magical little people who in ancient times were said to create things over night like the famous Menehune Pond in Lihue, Kauai. Though Hawaiians may not think much about the Menehune today, they do know the stories about them since these beliefs are part of the wider spirituality they embrace. This spirituality may include healing rites that are often associated with a Kahuna (Hawaiian healer), a belief in ghosts, and superstitions. In fact, this type of spirituality is something Hawaiians have in common with other Pacific Islanders as well as their strong sense of community and family interdependence, emphasis on oral history and genealogical traditions, a strong belief in harmony and balance to prevent conflict and outbursts of anger, and explicit roles based on age, gender, class, and ability (Weaver 2005, 197–99).

Like Hawaii, Guam has been very Americanized through colonization and as a territory of the United States since 1898. However, the island has a strong Roman Catholic tradition and it was under Japanese occupation during World War II. The indigenous people of Guam, which is the largest island of the Marianas, would be the descendents of the ancient Chamorros. Today they are a mixed ethnic group that has lost most of its original culture. However, Chamorros still have an indigenous identity socially and politically as they interact with other Chamorros on a regular basis, identify themselves as Chamorros first rather than Guamanian, and try to preserve some aspects of Chamorro culture such as language (Perez 2005).

Though Hawaii and Guam have had a strong U.S. presence with military bases on the islands, American Samoa has been more insulated from American influences. This is not to say that Samoa has been untouched by religious and other cultural influences from abroad. Samoans have been able to maintain traditional beliefs and practices despite these influences. Even when they come to California to set up residence there, they bring over these traditions and continue practicing them.

The rest of this chapter will focus on the history and culture of American Samoans as an example of a Pacific Island group that would require the building of trust before research could be done. As one of the larger Pacific Island groups to establish a community in Southern California, their culture includes a deep-seated spirituality complete with superstitions, folk healers, and oral traditions, as well as a strong sense of community and family and a very structured hierarchy of statuses complete with protocols of behavior. As you read about Samoan Americans in this chapter, you might get a feel for "native culture" even though many Samoans can outwardly appear assimilated.


## SAMOAN AMERICANS

### Introduction

The Samoan population in the South Bay area of Southern California became a large and visible community in the 1970s. Composed of members who began arriving on the West Coast since the U.S. naval facilities closed on American Samoa in the 1950s, Samoans have been coming over freely since then. Because American Samoa was incorporated into the United States Common-wealth as a trust territory in 1904, its residents are American nationals who can travel freely back and forth to the United States without being recorded by the U.S. Immigration and Naturalization Services (Shu and Satele 1977, 9). This makes it difficult to know how large the American Samoan population is in the United States. Immigrants from Western Samoa are recorded because this is an independent nation so there are population statistics on this group. However, because of immigration restrictions, one can assume that this group would be smaller in number than the population from American Samoa.

Over time, Samoans have spread to other parts of Southern California, includ-ing the Orange County area, but they are still concentrated in the South Bay area which is close to the campus of California State University–Dominguez Hills. Unlike other immigrant groups that rapidly assimilate to American cul-ture, Samoans are heavily embedded in an ancestral culture that is reinforced by strong kinship and community ties. This culture maintains itself through the continual influx of newcomers from Samoa who are immediate family members or members of a kin group. Family members who are already here will also send their children back to Samoa to live with kin so that the Samoan culture and way of life is preserved. In some ways this has resulted in an insular community creating an American or mainland-born generation that will adapt readily to American culture, but also be a part of a traditional society.

Some aspects of this traditional culture can be mentioned in this chapter to clarify the values and behaviors of these people. However, they are also important in understanding why Samoans may not trust the American ways of doing things and the American people who offer them services and also study them. Samoan culture is so different from Western culture that it may be dif-ficult to reconcile the value systems of both societies. It may lead to individu-als choosing one culture over the other in order to minimize conflict while living in American society. The culture can also be easily misunderstood or misrepresented, and this is why many Samoans do not have positive regard for Margaret Mead's early writings on Samoa.

## Aspects of Samoan Culture

The author visited American Samoa in the early 1980s when her brother was working there for the tuna industry. Though she only stayed for a week, she was very involved with the people and culture through her brother. Many of the impressions the author had of the culture and people coincided with what has been written about Samoans, but it was her brother who gave her the most useful information about how to behave around these people.

The author remembers going to a Samoan picnic for company employees and their families in American Samoa. This picnic began informally in the afternoon with chicken being barbecued and games being played in a park near the tuna processing factory. A woman brought the author a large quarter piece of grilled chicken to eat, and the author asked the woman if this was lunch. The woman said no, it was an appetizer. Later on everyone moved indoors for the actual meal and here is what it consisted of: a very large plate was presented to each guest that had big hunks of corned beef, ham, barbecued pig, taro root, and something wrapped in banana leaves. A second plate with side dishes came. Later on a third plate of several slices of cakes, pies, and cookies arrived. Now this would be enough food for an entire week! However, it was considered the usual amount that each guest is served at community events and festivities. It was enough food for a king and Samoans do want their guests to be lavished with food. Shu & Satele (1977, 20–21) might say this giving and receiving of food represents the Samoan value of being charitable and sharing what they have with others. The author saw it as an example of generosity.

American Samoa is an island with one major road that curves around the harbor of Pago Pago. Along this road is the town, and beyond the town is dense jungle. People live in villages presided over by matai (chiefs) on property owned by extended families and as members of a church that they will support financially and attend regularly. Because the habitable part of the island is small, everyone knows each other. They know where village property begins and ends and who the chiefs are. To the author, the neighborhoods do not look too different from each other. However, her brother would say we cannot go to that beach because it is owned by another village, and you have to ask permission from the chief before you can go there. As one can see, there is a formal hierarchy of positions within a village, and the village is comprised of extended families whose members share resources with each other generously. Church leaders also have high status within the community because the church is an important social institution within the community. The author attended Catholic mass on the island, though this is only one of the many Christian denominations in American Samoa.

Proper behavior within these tightly organized villages would imply putting the family first since the family owns property and accumulates goods and resources that get circulated among family members. The family lives with you, shares everything with you, stands by you, and gives protection (men), so in a way you are nothing without your family. The author's brother learned while in American Samoa that even when it comes to employee absenteeism, the family comes first. His employees were more likely to take off from work because of "family problems" than from being sick themselves. In the United States, this would not be an acceptable or common reason for employees to take off from work, but in American Samoa it is.

The family teaches the value of generosity to its children when they are very young. One might say that Samoan parents spoil their children by overindulging them with material things. However, the author would say that when children are given everything they ask for when they are little, they will also know how to give back to others, including their own children, when they are parents. Children do get what they ask for and this is also a way to make their bond very strong with parents. However, when Samoans are here on the mainland, this may be a family value that clashes with American values. An example of this comes to mind with a Samoan student. This woman took her younger brother and sister to Toys Я Us, and her siblings wanted several different types of toys. However, the student thought it wasn't right for the kids to get everything they asked for, so she only bought them one toy each. When they got home from the store, the little sister told their mother that she wasn't allowed to get all the things she wanted in the store. The mother reprimanded the student and told her to take the kids back to the store and buy them everything they wanted.

These children may appear spoiled by getting their material demands met. However, in a culture that emphasizes giving and sharing, hallmarks of generosity, they will later on start giving back to others, whether it is the traditional finemat given to guests and others on special occasions, or the giving of gifts and money to family members. It is within the family that cultural values such as these are passed on, so the family is extremely important in maintaining Samoan traditions. These traditions include folk remedies that are secrets within families and not told to outsiders, though Samoans may know how to heal in general using the plants and herbs within their natural environment on the island. On one occasion when the author was in American Samoa, she went to a beach with the author's niece, brother, and his Samoan friend. The niece was wading in the water but slipped and fell on a coral reef. She skinned her knee and it was bleeding. The Samoan man knew just what to do. He went to a bush and grabbed some leaves from it and rubbed the leaves together into a ball. Then he put the mixture on her knee; not only did it stop bleeding, but the deep scratches started to heal and disappear in just a few seconds. The author was very impressed at his knowledge but he did not reveal what kind of plant leaves he used. It was just something he learned in his family.

Samoans also learn in their family about causes of sickness and one of the causes can be by ghosts. Ghosts, however, are a taboo subject in Samoa. People do not talk about ghosts to outsiders because they are powerful spirits that can cause problems for the people. The world of spirits is very real for traditional Samoans even though they are members of Christian churches such as Mormon, Methodist, Catholic, and Pentecostal. With each family house having a cemetery in the front yard, it is not difficult to see how the dead remain close to the family all the time. This belief in ghosts and spirits of the deceased goes back to an earlier time way before Christianity came to the island in the 1800s, and it remains strong despite western influences.

Samoans are a warm, friendly, generous, and hospitable group of people who combine a Western look with very traditional cultural values. They do not show anger in public and do not like it when Westerners get openly upset and angry. The more traditional adults may wear sarongs and Polynesian-type clothes. However, the teenagers and younger people wear T-shirts and jeans. Though the dress code may appear flexible, it does not allow for bikinis on the beach. This was so highly frowned upon when the author was in American Samoa that a woman could get stoned by villagers for exposing her body this way. Even though Samoans may appear friendly and welcoming to outsiders and guests, a non-Samoan man should not assume that a friendly Samoan woman is being flirtatious and wants to have casual sex. According to the author's brother, sex is serious business on the island. If a man does have sex with a Samoan woman, it means that he wants to marry her. If he does not follow through with marriage, the woman's brothers will come after him to protect the woman's integrity.

These aspects of Samoan culture suggest that Samoans are adaptable when they come to the mainland, yet they are also very different in culture from the American ways of doing things. They will maintain aspects of traditional culture in their communities here because it eases their adjustment to American values. The male dominance continues here with the leadership roles of chiefs and church ministers. The Samoan language is prevalent in families and taught to children as well as the music, song and dances of Samoa. These arts are practiced over and over again here at ceremonies, festivities, celebrations and family events, keeping the culture alive for posterity.

Yet, one might say that this preservation of Samoan culture may slow assimilation down and make the people less likely to trust the American ways of doing things. They may also rely more heavily on the family and community for assistance, but this would quickly diminish their resources since they are coming from basically an agrarian society where there is little technology, to one that is highly technological and urban. This would mean that Samoans face discrepancies when they come here as a result of their low education and income, large families living under one roof, and lack of English skills. They may find it difficult to obtain employment, to adjust to schools, and to receive medical and mental health and other governmental services. The South Bay area does have social services for Samoans, but they may not be adequate in resolving the community problems that Shu and Satele (1977, 46) identified from their respondents, such as inadequate education, income, employment, housing, language barriers, problems in schools, and drinking problems.

On the other hand, even when adjustment problems are occurring with Samoans, it is important to see the benefits of cultural preservation and community solidarity. Though Samoan teenagers may suffer culture conflict, join gangs, abuse drugs and alcohol, run away from home and engage in delinquent acts, the community and family are still there to express concern for them and, they do try to resolve the problems. The church, especially, plays a strong role in supporting families and offering backup resources for them to use. The family also looks after the elderly quite well since they are given higher status in Samoan culture than in American society. Relying on the family and community leaders for help can be beneficial and comforting to an immigrant or migrant adjusting to an urban, high-technology society. The challenge for the Samoan American community is to balance traditional ways of doing things with more modern ways that include the use of outside services and agencies. In this way they will be able to advance in terms of education and occupation while maintaining a viable cultural heritage.

## Data from the Pilot Ethnic Research Training Project

Twenty Samoan respondents were interviewed by a Samoan informant/consultant and filled out questionnaires in 1980. The informant, who was fluent in Samoan, translated into English the eight questionnaires that were written in Samoan. The other twelve questionnaires were answered in English. The responses to these questionnaires and interviews can now be presented and analyzed in relationship to the cultural information described earlier.

## Attitude toward the University

All of the twenty Samoan respondents regarded higher education with great respect. It was not only considered an institution where one can broaden his wisdom and be enlightened, but also a place where one can learn good behavior and develop a vocational career. Respondents stated that American education is highly valued by Samoans because the schools in Samoa are not comparable to those here. Therefore, many Samoans come to the United States so they or their children can receive a better education.

As mentioned earlier, Samoans migrating to the mainland are coming over with low education, low incomes, and a lack of high technology skills. Competing with other immigrants and Americans for good paying jobs will be a challenge for Samoans, but they are realistic in knowing that the key to improving their socioeconomic status is to acquire a high education. They are also aware that the middle schools in the United States will give their children an advantage in competing at the higher levels of education, and this is one of the reasons why Samoans migrate to the United States. They want to give their children a better education than what they would receive in Samoa.

## Attitude toward Researchers

To many Samoans the researcher is regarded as an outsider or foreigner to their environment, but this does not mean his presence is not welcome. Researchers are known to sometimes come into the community to collect information or data on their culture or social structure, and they are sometimes regarded as "writers" or "historians." Some community members see the researcher as an observer whose research will help the people in some way. Therefore, they are highly regarded for the good name they might bring to the community. In all cases, they are welcome if their research does actually produce good results for the community. The Samoans are very sensitive about any research being done that will give them a bad name or make them appear negative or inferior in some way to outsiders. Therefore, they will be careful in how they convey data to a researcher.

In general, researchers could be thought of as special guests whom the people assume will do some good in the community, although some of the people remember Margaret Mead's work, which they regard unfavorably, and fear similar negative outcomes produced abut their community. Things that would make them look negative are statements that the people are on welfare or have criminal elements in the community or have loose sexual mores. Positive research is that which accurately conveys the traditions and the customs of the people. Only in a few cases would the Samoan people feel the researcher is spying on them, and these are usually instances where the research is not properly introduced or conducted.

To these respondents, a researcher is a role that could carry other names with it, such as "observer," "writer," and "historian." The role stands outside their culture and society, but as an imposition or intrusion into their way of life, it could have benefits. Like the person who is in the role of researcher, the role itself appears to be foreign or outside their community context. This may be why these respondents are not threatened by the researcher as "spy," but they are very concerned about his understanding of their culture and society, especially knowing what is appropriate or inappropriate to disclose. It is not enough that research be worthy to the researcher, it must fit the expectations of community members as well. The respondents are aware of the types of problems they have in the community and rather than having research disclose all their ills, they would want the researcher to create the conditions that would lead to an improvement in the community problems.

## Legitimate and Illegitimate Areas of Research

According to respondents, any area of research that would improve the Samoan community would be legitimate and welcome, but the area of education is especially needed and valued. This is because the community needs to find better ways of learning in order to "meet the challenge of living." Research on education would promote this progressive learning in the community and also provide bilingual education. Educational research is important in another sense. The youth are currently facing difficulties in American schools with language being the major problem. The Samoan people hope that research will help alleviate this problem and enable youth to speak the English language more fluently. By improving their education, the people hope that they will be able to solve their other problems.

Respondents mentioned other areas where research is needed. One of these is health, which is important to investigate because the people here are faced with many new diseases which they need to understand. They may also have problems adjusting to the Western medical system which includes medical treatment and hospitalization. One person mentioned research needed on hospitals, and a number of Samoans were interested in research on senior citizens because health is of major concern to the elderly. Old age and jobs were other areas mentioned consistently by respondents. Of lesser importance would be the area of social issues, though there is a need to do research on the Samoan social ranking system in the community which may be undergoing changes.

Areas or topics of research that are taboo and unwelcome have to do with one's private life, such as the subject of sex. Another highly taboo area is that of ghost beliefs and ghost sickness. This is a very personal area, and Samoans would fear negative consequences as a result of discussing these beliefs. Many of their medical beliefs and practices are highly taboo and not understood by outsiders, so they would not want to reveal them to nonfamily members. Some individuals also object to personal information being given out, such as occupation and income, which is asked in surveys, and they would not respond well on items asking about marital problems and crimes in the community.

In general, Samoans do not like to discuss any knowledge or topics that would end up ridiculing the people, and some of the areas above may have a tendency to do so in terms of the foreigner's conceptions.

Consistent with community problems mentioned earlier by respondents, education and language barriers stand out as areas that need attention. However, it is not just bilingual education that is needed; it is knowledge about American society with its complex system of rules and norms, services and bureaucratic systems, and windows of opportunity for jobs and education. There is an ongoing need to learn about American society in order to adapt to the culture and understand the subject matter in schools so that one gets good grades. If researchers studied how Samoans could improve their language and educational skills, there would be little resistance by the Samoan people.

On the other hand, doing research in the medical area may not be as easy to accomplish. Even though respondents saw a need for research on health and disease, including medical treatment and hospitalization, Samoans would not be willing to talk about their medical beliefs and practices because they are personal and very different from Western beliefs. They include the earlier mentioned ghost beliefs and ghost sickness which are taboo to discuss.

Samoans are likely to get new diseases when they migrate here, and they will need to consult with American doctors and health care practitioners. They will be asked what treatments they are currently using and the medicines they are taking. Normally, they will be given drugs that hopefully will not interact with any herbs they are taking or other home remedies. However, if they believe that an illness is caused by ghosts and the patient does not get better with Western treatment, Samoans may not trust the American system of medicine. They are likely to revert back to the folk healers in their community who understand these illnesses and the Samoan treatment and rituals to appease the ghosts.

As one can see, research can be more problematic with Samoans than with more acculturated ethnic groups, and this may have a lot to do with how different the culture is from that of the United States. There may be a desire on the part of the community for more research information on a specific topic. However, getting the full cooperation of respondents may be difficult to achieve without trust given the taboo nature of certain subjects and the discomfort of revealing things that may have negative consequences for the people.

## Participation in Research

When it comes to getting involved in any type of research, most of the respondents wanted to first know the purpose or objective of the research in detail; and then to be informed of all aspects of it. This knowledge about the research would prevent them from being misled or misinformed. They were also concerned about knowing which community members would be selected for participation in the research. Apparently, they wanted to carefully guide the researcher in selecting suitable participants. This concern stems from their desire to have members of the community who are highly regarded by the people consulted first, even though there are many different social-religious networks in the community. Should there be anything objectionable about the research, Samoans would want to express this to the researcher. The respondents were able to mention a few things that would offend them when research is being done in their community. They are summarized in the following list:

1. Conducting research without the community knowing about it or understanding its purpose
2. Being misled about research objectives
3. Publishing anything negative about the community
4. Making observations in the community without spending an adequate amount of time there, and using these observations to form conclusions which may be misleading

These concerns about research that the Samoan respondents have imply that others do not understand them and their culture very well. They, in turn, may not understand American culture that well, so that there is always a chance of being perceived incorrectly by Westerners and of Samoans misunderstanding Americans. Under these circumstances, it would be easy for Samoans to not trust the outsider who does not know the Samoan ways well enough to respect their norms and to form conclusions about them through research. If researchers do come into the community, they require careful monitoring by Samoan leaders.

## Expected Behavior toward Community Members

According to respondents, the Samoan community has a definite social structure made up of various ranks of people. This hierarchy includes high chiefs and ministers at the top, high talking chiefs below them, common talking chiefs (all of whom are men), women, and children. The researcher is cautioned to be aware that this hierarchy exists, and when approaching members of the Samoan community should enter through the leaders who are the chiefs and ministers. Behavior toward these members requires formality and respect and knowing the proper terms to use in addressing the higher ranks of community members. These forms of address are described in the following chart.

**Table 10.1.   Samoan Community Hierarchy (The Matai Political Structure)**

| Rank | Title | Address |
|------|-------|---------|
| 1 | High Chief = Leader or head of village whose role is that of advisor or peacemaker | afioga |
| (1) | (Minister = Religious leader and usually the leader of the Samoan community here because the matai structure is diffuse.) | (susuga) |
| 2 | High Talking Chief = Leader of the village who represents the people in policy making. | tofa |
| 3 | Common Talking Chief = An individual of title who has no specific function in the community, though he may act in the High Talking Chief's place during his absence. | tofa |

(The women have no community rank though their status is significant in the women's community organizations. The numbers used are merely to point out levels of social status.)

| | | |
|------|-------|---------|
| 4 | Chief or minister's wife | faletua |
| 5 | High talking chief and common talking chief's wife | tausi |
| 6 | women (in general) | tama' itai |

With women and younger children there is no definite standard of behavior that the researcher should use other than being friendly and courteous toward them, but the wives of the chiefs must be respected in the same way as their husbands. Other nonranking adults in the community should be acknowledged in a respectful manner as well, though no specific titles would be used to address them.

The elders of the community are highly respected, and in some cases their status would overlap with the high-ranking leaders of the community. Young men are ranked below the male leaders of the community although males, in general, have higher status than females. Children should be addressed last, and they will usually be courteous and respectful toward foreigners.

When first entering the Samoan house, respondents pointed out that the researcher should sit down, cross-legged, and properly acknowledge the community or all the people present. This is called addressing the community to whom the honor is due or acknowledging the community on its own behalf. From here one pays respect to each of the ranking members of the community. If it is a religious community, the acknowledgements go from the faifeau (minister), to the tiakono (deacon), to the faletua (minister's wife), and from there to the church as a whole. If it is a politically-organized community group or social event, one must start with the high chief, then the high talking chief, the common talking chief, and then the community as a whole.

Before one acknowledges the community, though, one must first have permission to do the research from the leaders who will welcome the stranger to the community. In order to find out who the leaders are, the researcher should ask for direction from other members of the community. One way to tell who they are is to study the seating arrangement of the house. The chiefs will sit to the right or the left of the house, while other members of the family or community will sit behind them and in back of the house. Also, the place settings at the table will show the status and rank of community members with the chiefs having more elaborate place settings.

By now it should be clear to the reader that the Samoan community still uses traditional forms of address toward members based on status. This ranking system is still an important part of Samoan culture, and it illustrates the way ancestral traditions can persist despite the forces of assimilation and technological development in American society. Though the matai political structure may be undergoing changes in the United States, it still exists in American and Western Samoa. With the constant flow of migration and immigration from the two Samoas reinforcing the matai political structure here, it is not likely to disappear that quickly.

Because of the wide difference between American and Samoan culture, it will be more challenging for the researcher to display proper behavior in this community than in other ethnic communities. Proper forms of address in the Samoan language may need to be learned as well as proper etiquette when contacting Samoan leaders. The author made the mistake of calling a Samoan chief on the telephone when he had already sat down to dinner. Though the chief was willing to give the author a brief interview, she could clearly see that he was offended by the interruption of his meal.

### Customs and Community Traditions to Observe

Respondents felt that the researcher should attempt to learn the Samoan language so that he/she can use the proper forms of address to the leaders of the community and be able to interact with the various people there. He should also know the relationship between males and females, parents and children, matai and young men and how to behave toward each of these groups.

The researcher should know the term "matai" (which means the head of the household or family) and how each matai is ranked in the community. This is where the system of chiefs and a status hierarchy come in. Within the family there is also a social structure, as pointed out earlier, of which the researcher should be aware.

The researcher should also note that within the community there is both a religious and a political order which are kept separate. The religious social structure is very important because the Samoans center their social lifestyle on religion. The priest is the head of this order, and he has a great influence upon the people. He is not only a religious leader but a social leader as well, being dominant in community affairs. This is a good person to contact if one is doing research with the Samoan community. Most types of research should follow this route since the religious community is more obvious than the political community. This latter involves the system of high chiefs and talking chiefs, and one should approach the leader of this community when doing research on the family system and community structure.

### SUMMARY

Though the Samoan American community may be difficult to study because of cultural differences from the United States, it provides a wonderful opportunity to see how a once tightly-knit group is going through changes as the people adapt to American society. Since the traditional Samoan culture is still intact in many ways, it can be studied both sociologically and anthropologically, or in terms of social norms and behavior changes, or with a focus on culture. Another interesting way of studying the Samoan ethnic group is to compare it with the Mexican American group in terms of cultural retention. Both groups have a high rate of visitation to their ancestral land and they manage to maintain their culture and identity despite the strong forces of assimilation. Though Samoans have a different history here in the United States from Mexican Americans, they do retain their language with the younger generation even as these children and teenagers rapidly assimilate to American ways.

Unlike Mexican Americans, though, Samoans have a culture that is not that familiar to Americans. It is a culture that is kept within the family and the Samoan community, so Americans would not have access to it unless they visited the homes of Samoans or went to American Samoa. This culture would pose many challenges for the researcher because it has a formal structure of authority that includes both religious and political leaders in the community and a hierarchy within the family. Knowing whom to contact first and how to address individuals would require some training. Knowing what topics to discuss and what topics to avoid would require additional skills in order to access reliable data. Perhaps the most basic thing about these cultural challenges for the researcher is establishing trust with the people.

With Samoans, the need for trust relates to their desire for cultural understanding and an accurate perception of who they are as a people. Since they do not have a long history in the United States as an ethnic group, they have not built up distrust through generations of racial discrimination and prejudice like other ethnic groups have. However, Samoans have experienced negative attitudes and treatment from others because they are Samoan, and some of it has had serious consequences for them. These experiences could lead to distrust, as well, for individuals, but the cultural differences are likely to have a greater ramification on Samoan families and communities. The more foreign the culture is, the greater the need for understanding in order to adapt to each other's differences. In this context, trust would come with cultural receptivity, especially on the part of the researcher.

Unlike other Pacific Islanders, Samoans who have come to the United States still retain a good deal of their traditional culture. It may not be obvious to others that this culture exists, but it would show up with service providers and agencies as they interact with the Samoan community and try to work with the unmet needs of the people. There are books on service delivery to ethnic populations, especially in the social work, health, and mental health fields, to further guide researchers on approaching Samoan and other Pacific Island people. While they are useful, it is also a good idea to look deeper at a Pacific Islander and know that traditional beliefs may still be there despite the more obvious signs of assimilation that have taken place.

## *Part IV*

In this final chapter, one can find a deeper analysis of the process of under-standings and interactions that lead to the building of trust. Theoretically ethnic groups need to be understood in terms of their experience in the United States as well as the retention of their traditional culture. Positive and nega-tive experiences form the basis for understanding the development of trust which leads to insights about behaviors that could be used to correct the lack of trust. Formed as recommendations for the researcher, these behaviors are provided separately for each ethic group studied in the Pilot Ethnic Research Training Project.

A final summary reinforces the need for carefully constructed pre-meth-odology strategies for use in ethnic communities. As a way to build trust between researcher and ethnic members, these strategies show how the social sciences can be of service to the ethnic community as they model positive relationships that others can learn from and practice.

# *Chapter 11*

# Building Trust

Building trust with people is so important in relationships that it is the basic premise of this book that fieldwork success in ethnic communities cannot occur without this trust. However, trust is something that needs to be built up since it is not automatically there among strangers, and it is much less likely to be there in larger cities than in smaller towns. The challenge for the researcher is to know how to build trust with members of an ethnic group that are selected for study. The chapters presented earlier were developed to show the unique historical and cultural features of different ethnic groups as their views toward researchers and research being conducted in their communities were examined. After reading these chapters, one might conclude that these ethnic groups do have different expectations for the researcher and different needs within their communities. This would imply that trust would have to be built up differently with each ethnic group as one pays attention to their specific history, culture, and their perception of problems that deserve study. Along these lines, this chapter will develop a perspective on building trust that will be applied to the various ethnic groups who participated in the Pilot Ethnic Research Training Project. This perspective should also be useful to the study of other groups in society and hopefully it will open many doors for the researcher.

## THEORETICAL FRAMEWORK

Based on the data collected earlier from the Southeast Asians, African Americans, Japanese Americans, Mexican Americans, and Samoan Americans, the issue of intergroup trust or mistrust seems to be related to two factors. These two factors are ethnic group acceptance and cultural understanding. When trust is related to ethnic group acceptance, then distrust would occur when there is prejudice and discrimination over a long historical period. The group in power is likely to be distrusted by minority groups who were not treated fairly by the dominant group because of their race or ethnicity. The minority groups are seeking acceptance on an equal basis with other groups, and if they receive it, then trust will follow. When trust is related to cultural understanding, then distrust occurs when people feel they are not being understood for who they are as a people or ethnic group. They see others treating them in an insensitive way and being ignorant of proper ways to behave in their culture. In both cases, the behavior of others is defined negatively, which leads to mistrust.

As mentioned in previous chapters, the issue of trust affects ethnic relations and the conflict that can develop between groups. Fueled by the forces of racism with its consequences of prejudice and discrimination, a lack of trust creates divisions between people that get reinforced by the negative beliefs and actions that groups constantly display toward each other. On the other hand, trust would tend to bring people together in cooperative ways, and if the behaviors are perceived as positive, then trust gets reinforced. When individuals are doing fieldwork in ethnic communities, they are offered a valuable opportunity to participate in the building of trust. As researchers, they will have to interact with their respondents face-to-face and acquire information about them that may be personal, in depth, and extensive. Unlike the collection of statistical survey data, researchers doing fieldwork have the opportunity to understand the actual day-to-day relations and encounters between people of different ethnic backgrounds that help to build interethnic trust relations (Matejko and Williams 1993).

Before going out to an ethnic community, however, it is important that researchers study the history of relationships between the ethnic group and the dominant society. With ethnic minorities in the United States, this information is readily available through textbooks. With recent immigrants to the United States, the history of the nation the group has left behind is important to study in order to see the power struggles that affected the group. The reason for acquiring this information is to see if earlier distrust existed with the ethnic group because of this inequality in group relations. Theoretically, if distrust develops because of unequal treatment by the dominant group, then a different type of action would be necessary to build trust than if the reason for distrust is due to cultural misunderstanding.

When distrust occurs because ethnic groups are not accepted, the building of trust would require contact first and then interaction on an equal basis. This is related to LaPiere's (1934) belief that contact reduces prejudice which, in turn, reduces discrimination. As individuals from diverse groups interact, they become more familiar with each other, and it is this familiarity that leads to confidence in the other and a predictability of the other's actions; both of which lead to trust (Welch et al. 2005, 460). As interaction continues, it is possible for individuals to see similarities between themselves in interests, identities, and values and they may begin to see that it is in their own self-interest to trust the other person (Ibid., 461).

To build up this trust would require opportunities to get involved with an ethnic community that did not have a voice before and that lacked power to influence others with their needs. Murry and Brody (2004) had the right idea when they studied rural African American families intensively before instituting an agency program to treat substance abuse and sexual activity among youth. They specifically used focus groups to identify ethnic group concerns about the family service intervention model they planned to implement in the community. Focus groups are usually done in the beginning of more extensive data collection to get a feel for a community. However, they can just as easily be used to begin the interaction process with an ethnic community that does not trust researchers. When researchers from the dominant group show interest in an ethnic group's concerns and problems and are willing to learn from them, this will break down some of the barriers of inequality. As the interaction continues with ongoing input from the ethnic community in the dominant group's research, the trust can begin to develop. Trust takes a while to develop, especially if distrust between groups has a long history. According to Matejko and Williams (1993), inter-ethnic trust comes about when formal and informal groups share cooperative tasks over a period of time where there is mutual dependence and consultation.

On the other hand, when interethnic distrust occurs because of cultural misunderstanding, a different strategy is in order. The more cultures differ from each other, the more foreign they appear and individuals are more likely to display ethnocentrism toward each other rather than prejudice and discrimination. Ethnocentrism exists when group members feel that its cultural beliefs, traditions, and values are superior to those of another group, and they are likely to discount the importance of the other group's culture. Though ethnocentrism can exist with both groups that are different from each other, the dominant group's ethnocentrism may take the form of imposing its cultural views on the subordinate group because these views are considered superior to those of the subordinate group. The latter group, in turn, may distrust the dominant group because it is trying to change its valued heritage, or it is not acknowledging its culture in appropriate ways.

The solution to this type of distrust is for the dominant group to learn about a group's culture and to demonstrate knowledge of this culture when interacting with the ethnic members. This can be done in various ways. The easiest way is to read up about the group's culture before venturing out into their community. There are many textbooks written on the different types of ethnic groups that live in Southern California, so this is a good place to start. Another way to minimize distrust due to cultural differences is to use members from the ethnic community that one wishes to study in the research process. When consultants or informants are of the same ethnicity as the ethnic group being studied, you are showing respect for the culture and approaching the community in a culturally syntonic or harmonious way (Muir et al. 2004). By using these ethnic consultants and depending on them for insight into the group's culture, the researcher not only builds interethnic trust but also prevents the rejection of new ideas that may be useful to the ethnic group. A classic example of where rejection did occur is in Clyde Kluckhohn and Dorothea Leighton's ethnography, *The Navajo* (1962), where western health ideas were rejected because Navajo values were not understood.

There is a saying that people do not like to change old ways of doing things. If we were to apply this to culture, then the old ways would be the traditions, values, and behaviors that we learned from our families. Many of these old ways are taken for granted by us, and we are not even conscious that we are following old ways of doing things. All we know is that change can be disruptive and, in dramatic form, can even be traumatic. If people get to know our culture first before they try to implement change, then change is less likely to be threatening and traumatic. It makes individuals more willing to take risks, and it builds up trust between insider and outsider.

The author is a marriage and family therapist who specializes in cross-cultural couple counseling. Now this is an area that is rife with cultural misunderstandings that not only can lead to distrust between partners but also the dissolution of marriages. In the beginning, though, individuals may be physically and socially attracted to each other, and this may lead to a relationship. Matejko and Williams (1993) would say that a long series of compromises from both partners can emerge where constant negotiations are made and cultural exchanges take place. This is in the ideal situation. Many times, partners from different ethnic backgrounds begin to distrust each other soon after the honeymoon when more serious negotiations and major decisions need to be made. The distrust is greater, the more foreign or different the two cultures are. Therefore, it is not surprising that there is a high divorce rate among interethnic couples, and this is probably due to the inability of partners to negotiate cultural differences in long-term relationships.

When cross-cultural couples begin to work on their relationship in therapy, they begin to see how their expectations of each other are culturally tinged. Many times a partner's way of seeing things and doing things is based on values learned within a cultural context that made sense to the individual when he/she was growing up, but in a cross-cultural context these values may not work. They need to be negotiated rather than imposed on the partner or taken for granted. Couples can fight over disagreements anyway, but when you add on the cultural differences as well, the relationship can be very difficult to handle. Therapy helps the partners see and understand the cultural differences so that they can manage them better. In this way they are able to learn to trust their partner again as they make compromises.

At a macro level, these cultural conflicts are visible in our society when two or more ethnic groups are living in close proximity, and they are in competition for scarce resources. The African American and Korean conflict in Los Angeles several years ago is a case in point where violence erupted and created hostilities between the groups. At the heart of this conflict was distrust between the groups because of cultural differences. This was not a case of inequality leading to unfair treatment, because both groups have felt oppression from the dominant group, and both groups in this area had lower socioeconomic status. In this situation, a Korean convenience store owner shot to death an African American teenager that she thought was shoplifting from her store. This incident sparked outrage from the African American community and a long-term animosity that only started to get better when community leaders from both ethnic groups began to make contact with each other and encourage the exchange of culture between the two communities. These efforts lead to festivals in Los Angeles where music, dance, and food were introduced in an attempt to get cultural understanding. By having these community events, people were able to come together and learn about each other's ways. This, of course, is a way to build trust by learning about another group's culture.

The building of trust requires some interaction between people and knowledge of whether the distrust is due to cultural misunderstanding or a failure to accept a group on an equal basis. Though these two factors have been described as two separate entities, they can both be at work in the same interethnic relationship. In other words, it is possible for a group to be treated unequally and also be misunderstood for its culture, and both of these reasons could lead to distrust.

By now it should be clear to the reader that contact in itself does not reduce prejudice and build trust, though it may reduce discrimination if the norms are in place against discrimination. To build trust, the following theory is offered as an interactional process that develops over time.

1. Individuals from different ethnic/racial groups must have continual contact and interaction to build up knowledge about each other.
2. If this knowledge is viewed positively, then more interaction will be sought because it is rewarding rather than costly. This is a principle from Homans' (1958) social exchange theory.

3. As contact continues between members of different ethnic groups, both past history with negative memories and cultural misperceptions may still arise. The desire to continue interacting occurs because individuals can weigh the pros and cons of interaction with the other person. If the pros are higher than the cons, then interaction will continue.

4. As behaviors become predictable and viewed as positive, individuals begin to learn trust. This is Erikson's (1950) first stage of psychosocial development for the infant. It is mentioned here at the end because it is through a process of re-learning that people start to trust others as adults. Erikson describes the general state of trust in the following way: "not only that one has learned to rely on the sameness and continuity of the outer providers, but also that one may trust oneself and the capacity of one's own organs to cope with urges" (1950, 248).

This theory would fit the earlier hypothesis formed in chapter 5 that groups who have experienced more negative treatment by the host society historically should exhibit more distrust of researchers, than those groups who have had less negative treatment. Based on this theory of trust building, the following section will look at the different groups studied in the Pilot Ethnic Research training Project to see where distrust is most evident. Guidelines for creating trust with each group will be provided as they encourage behaviors that conform to the theory.

## UNDERSTANDING DISTRUST IN ORDER TO BUILD UP TRUST

Each of the ethnic groups presented earlier in the book had certain views about researchers and research being done in their community. These views were analyzed in terms of the group's cultural background and history. The problems that each ethnic group identified for its community were also presented so that the reader could see what the group's needs were as respondents thought about how research could benefit them. Based on all the respondents' comments, a set of recommendations can now be made for each group that should be helpful to the fieldworker who is trying to adapt to the ethnic community. These fieldwork recommendations will form the basis for discussing distrust in ethnic relations and the way that trust can be built up.

### Southeast Asians

Based on the questionnaire interviews that were done with Southeast Asians, a number of recommendations can be made about how to do research in these communities. They are broken down according to the following three ethnic groups: the Lao, Vietnamese, and Chinese Vietnamese.

## Lao

1. Have someone introduce you to the Lao family. Do not introduce your-self.
2. Go through the head of household before interviewing family members.
3. Be properly dressed.
4. Socialize with the respondent first before conducting the interview.
5. Be observant of cultural customs.

## Vietnamese

1. Be careful in selecting a topic, making sure that sensitive questions are not asked.
2. Socialize with the respondent first.
3. Ask questions in a roundabout fashion rather than in a direct way.
4. Be polite and reserved in manners.
5. Accept food and beverages offered by the hostess or host.

## Chinese Vietnamese

1. Notify respondents formally before coming to interview them.
2. State questions clearly and in simple language. Do not use sophisticated words or lengthy sentences.
3. Have a neat appearance.
4. Show respect for the elderly.
5. Be polite and respectable.
6. Keep the interview brief.

With the Southeast Asian ethnic groups, one can see mistrust being strongly related to cultural differences and the lack of understanding this would pro-duce. All three groups—the Lao, Vietnamese and Vietnamese Chinese—are concerned about the researcher's proper behavior when doing research in their ethnic communities, so the recommendations made above are basically to educate the researcher about these groups' cultures. In this way, Southeast Asians would be able to build trust in the researcher.

However, with the Vietnamese and Chinese Vietnamese groups, there has been interethnic conflict between them and Americans during the Vietnam War, resulting in prejudice and discrimination toward the Vietnamese when they came here as refugees. The United States would be viewed as the superior power that invaded Vietnam even though they did not win the war. As a result of this history, the Vietnamese who are here may distrust Americans because they have not been accepted as an ethnic group with equal rights. This type of distrust would require contact to reduce the prejudice on both sides, and some of the recommendations mentioned above would be useful here. For example, socializing with the respondents first before asking research questions, and asking questions in a roundabout fashion rather than directly, would help individuals become acquainted. Doing a lot of socializing before starting the interview would be beneficial since this is a way to establish rapport and begin to see the "other" in a more positive light.

## AFRICAN AMERICANS

The following set of recommendations can be made about doing research in African American communities. They are based on the responses from community members that were presented in chapter 7:

1. Select a topic for study that would be of interest to the community people rather than one that has already been researched by social scientists.
2. Whenever you can, use African Americans as consultants to help you identify research problems and interpret results.
3. Know the best time of day to interview respondents.
4. Avoid preconceptions about African Americans based on other people's research findings. Go in with an unbiased perspective.
5. Be open to the perspectives of the people.
6. Be sincere and respectful in manners, not overly casual, and friendly with an extreme effort to please. Acting familiar is a sign of condescension.
7. Learn the vocabulary of the people and their social cues along the way.

The type of distrust that these recommendations reveal about African Americans is the one based on the need for group acceptance. African Americans do not have a foreign culture that would cause distrust; in fact, they are as Americanized as the dominant group. However, they have had a long history of oppression in the United States since the days of slavery, when they had no rights as human beings, to their current state of experiencing ongoing prejudice and discrimination from others. These recommendations would solve some of the problems of inequality between African Americans and the researcher because they are focusing on the needs of this ethnic group.

African Americans see the problems in their community as a result of unequal opportunities for their members, and they show up in areas such as education, employment, housing, and recreation. When a researcher listens to them and does research on these practical problems, trust can be built. African Americans are also sensitive about earlier research that has been done on them that resulted in negative stereotypes about the group; specifically, on topics such as African American poverty, crime, family instability, and unemployment. The public may already know these things through the media so what is the point of repeating them? Research should go way beyond just identifying problems to finding solutions to problems that are embedded in unequal treatment and racism. Being open to the perspectives of the people, using African Americans as consultants in research, and being sincere and respectful are other ways to build trust among the people.

## Japanese Americans

Research recommendations for Japanese Americans can be presented as follows:

1. Before beginning your research, have a member of the community introduce you or have your research announced in local papers.
2. Explain how your study will be of benefit to the respondent or the community people.
3. Don't expect your respondents to be "foreign" or speak Japanese. Even the second generation elderly can have perfect command of the English language. Find out what generation they are before assuming their degree of ethnicity.
4. Behave with varying degrees of formality or casualness depending on the receptivity of the respondent. Variations in approach should depend on how Western the respondent is.
5. Be respectful of the elderly and their traditional ways.

With Japanese Americans who are older and more traditional, there may be some distrust based on cultural differences. However, with the majority of Japanese Americans, there is more a concern about being treated as foreigners by the larger society even though they are quite assimilated. This concern relates to distrust based on the lack of ethnic group acceptance. As mentioned in chapter 8, Japanese Americans have had a history of being viewed as outsiders, as foreign, and as the enemy on American soil. Their mass evacuation into America's concentration camps during World War II made them realize that they could not trust the dominant group when it came to basic rights and equal treatment. The dominant group, in turn, justified the internment of Japanese Americans by saying they could not trust these people who would side with Japan during the war. This distrust on the part of Japanese Americans further manifests itself in their lack of receptivity to a researcher unless he or she is first introduced by a member of the community.

To build up trust with Japanese Americans, the researcher could begin by identifying the older and more traditional Japanese who require more cultural understanding and follow the cultural dictates presented in chapter 8 when interacting with them. With other Japanese Americans, trust would need to be built through acceptance and this would take longer to establish. It is important that the researcher find a Japanese American to introduce him to the community before he starts interviewing people there. Even though Japanese Americans are assimilated and understand the nature of academic research, they would not be comfortable with a stranger imposing himself on them. They would also want to know about the research, and this type of discussion would create equality in the interaction between researcher and ethnic respondents. Acceptance also means treating the Japanese American as another American rather than a foreigner. One should not assume that Japanese Americans are from Japan, speak Japanese, eat Japanese food, or are "model minorities." Japanese Americans may or may not be highly educated and have good jobs, but they probably have experienced some negative treatment where they were seen as "different." Trust can be built with Japanese Americans when they see that others regard them as trustworthy Americans.

## Mexican Americans

The Mexican American community is diverse and includes both recent immigrants from Mexico and highly assimilated individuals whose families have been here for generations. The following recommendations for researchers do not separate these two populations, but they are useful in a general sense:

1. Have a community member introduce you to respondents, especially if they are more traditional Mexican Americans.
2. Explain your research purpose carefully, stressing the need for respondent cooperation and how it will benefit the people. Show how the study is worthy of their time.
3. Introduce yourself as a person from the university doing a "study" rather than a "research project." Show your credentials.
4. Shake hands with family members and greet the male first. Formal introductions are important.
5. Adapt to the mood of the people and the atmosphere of the home. Socializing and casual conversation may be expected before the interview.

6. Show openness and spontaneity in your behavior.
7. Learn the customs, history, and language of the people if you can, but don't use them merely to make an impression on the people.

With Mexican Americans, trust may require both cultural understanding and group acceptance. However, the group acceptance would be more important with this population because the public sees this group as having illegal immigrants that they may not welcome here. The public is also more familiar with Mexican culture because of its lasting heritage in Los Angeles and the Southwest, so they are more likely to be aware of traditional expectations.

The distrust that Mexican Americans feel toward outsiders can be seen in the need for proper introductions through a community member and for the researcher showing his or her credentials. They want to be sure that the researcher is really an academic person doing an "educational study" rather than an "experiment" where they are used as guinea pigs. They would especially be suspicious if this person worked for the government and was trying to deport them back to Mexico. By being properly introduced to the community and showing his credentials, the researcher will be able to build trust with Mexican Americans.

Other ways of building trust include learning the customs, history, and language of the people so that there is greater cultural understanding, socializing with the respondents before the interview, and discussing the research purpose after the socializing so that there is equality in interaction. As mentioned earlier, group acceptance comes from contact, and this contact should be ongoing to reduce prejudice and discrimination. The more people socialize with each other and discuss research openly and spontaneously, the more trusting they will be of the other person's motives. The "other" person should also be able to learn more about the ethnic members so that acceptance becomes easier for him or her as well.

## Samoan Americans

The following fieldwork recommendations can be made for Samoans:

1. Be careful of the research topic you select. If your hypothesis implies anything negative or harmful about the group, do not use it. If in doubt, consult with Samoan community members to find out how they feel about your research topic.
2. Go through a matai or minister when introducing your research study to the community. If you do not know a matai or minister, ask someone in the community to introduce you to one.

3. Avoid asking questions directly that are personal, that is, questions on income and occupation, or use discretion in asking these questions.
4. Speak to the oldest person first when addressing a large group.
5. Be observant of the status and title of family and community members, that is, high chief, high talking chief, common talking chief.
6. Do not ask people for family names. They are reluctant to disclose them to strangers for fear of being exploited.
7. Keep people informed of research activities throughout the project's operation, and invite their participation.
8. Be tolerant of Samoan cultural beliefs and views on medicine. Beliefs about the supernatural are taken seriously by the people and should be respected.

These recommendations are clearly concerned with cultural violations and ways to prevent them. As mentioned in chapter 10, Samoan culture is very different from American culture and this in itself can lead to instances of cultural conflict. The conflicts can lead to misunderstandings between people that, in turn, lead to distrust. The solution to this type of distrust is to develop knowledge of the culture and proper observance of some of the practices.

It is a good idea to read up about the Samoan culture and history before going out into a Samoan community. However, be prepared for experiences that may not conform to what is written. The author's suggestion is to find Samoan American students at a university or community college in the area of the ethnic community to help one gain access to the leaders of the community who are likely to be ministers or matai. Since students are usually younger and more assimilated than their parents, they make access to a Samoan community much easier than if one goes there alone. They are also more trusting of Americans and researchers who do not appear as foreign to them as they would to the older generation of Samoans. Once this is done, the researcher can proceed to meet the leaders of the community and introduce his research project to them.

As mentioned in the first recommendation, the research topic should not be stated in a way that would imply that there is a problem in the Samoan community that needs to be fixed. It is better to introduce a research project by stating how it can benefit a community or the ethnic group. This would be true for research done in any ethnic community. Samoans rightfully do not want to be described in negative ways by a researcher's findings so it is important to generate a positive hypothesis about a research problem or topic. If the researcher can get this far with Samoan leaders, then he is already building up some trust with them. Once the leader (i.e., Samoan minister) approves the research project, getting respondents becomes much easier.

The minister may simply let the researcher come to his church to administer questionnaires.

Trust can be further built when the researcher avoids asking questions that are too personal or that are taboo, that is, asking about family medicines or beliefs about ghosts. There are plenty of other topics that can be discussed before going into areas that may be sensitive to Samoans, and the rule of thumb is to proceed slowly and cautiously into these areas. It helps if the researcher knows who the chiefs are so that they are addressed properly, as well as knowing the status hierarchy in the family when approaching members. Observing these formalities and others will build trust with Samoans. It is basically the researcher joining in with the Samoan culture that makes him a welcome guest to the community because it implies that he is willing to learn from the people. They would be even more trusting when the researcher keeps the people informed of the research throughout its duration and also has them participate as informants or consultants. This means that they have more say about the outcome of the research and have more influence over the research report's accuracy.

## SUMMARY

Despite the fact that there are vast cultural differences between ethnic groups and varying modes of their adaptation to American society, there are proper courtesies each group would like to have observed by those outside their group. These courtesies would help to build up both types of trust: that based on cultural understanding and that based on group acceptance.

1. *Proper Introduction by a Community Member*: It is logical to assume that if a friend introduces a person to his friend, this person will be more likely to get acquainted with the stranger than if he made the introduction on his own. In sociological terms, an individual will feel some obligation to treat the stranger with courtesy because he/she is the friend of a friend and, therefore, a potential member of one's acquaintance circle.
2. *Informing Individuals about the Study*: People want to be aware of activities that affect them. If an interviewer does research in a community, respondents should know why they are being interviewed.
3. *Being Knowledgeable about Taboo Areas*: Each group had specific areas of research that were sensitive for them. For many it was answering questions related to sex or family difficulties. These areas should be handled very carefully by the researcher.
4. *Researching Areas that Ethnic Members Consider Relevant*: Ethnic members will have areas that concern them that need solution or study. To the

researcher, these may not be areas of his concern, but if he wishes to study the community more accurately, he would do well to identify problems in line with the way the people see them.

5. *Showing Sincerity, Honesty, and Trustworthiness*: No minority member would feel comfortable around a researcher if he/she displays anything less than this. Community members have many times been harassed by census takers, social workers, health personnel, immigration officials, and many other types of agents who were not always sympathetic to them. The researcher should make sure that he does not get placed in the same category as these people.

6. *Showing Respect for the Elderly*: Many ethnic groups value their elderly in ways that are unfamiliar to Westerners. The elderly have a place in the household and community, and these are positions that are highly respected.

7. *Accepting Community Hospitality*: This includes partaking of food and beverages and socializing with respondents before starting the interview.

8. *Making Research Results Known to Community Members*: Many ethnic members want to see how changes can come about in their community, especially if the researcher is working on a problem of concern to them. It is good practice to inform respondents, in some way, of one's research findings especially if they request it.

Ethnic members have been the subject of studies for many centuries now, being the topic of tourist observations and the focus of missionary reports. Social scientists, too, have done their share of research on the minority group by developing theories about the people and publishing data on their group characteristics. What has been lacking, though, is the input of the ethnic people themselves in research findings. It is as though they were always the alienated subject in a project designed to treat them as objects rather than human beings. Rarely have they been thought of as having a perspective of their own, or feelings and emotions real enough to be counted. Yet, ethnic people have their needs and problems and they desire very much to communicate these to others. As a group, they are aware of their situation in American society, and they very much want studies to benefit them as well as the researcher. What they need least of all is more dictatorial treatment and stereotyped perceptions that will oppress them further.

A solution to this problem is for researchers and fieldworkers to become aware of ethnic members as valuable research informants or consultants. In order for this to happen, researchers must go into the community with a new way of perceiving the people—one where they are thought of as research partners who can help the researcher find answers to questions that are both community and academically relevant. Too often the researcher approaches people with an air of superiority that community members are quick to notice and that prevents them from trusting or liking the researcher. What is needed is a type of collaborative research between researcher and community members that enables the people to participate in research not only at the very beginning but throughout the project to its completion and dissemination of results. Joan Moore's effort with Mexican American gang members and ex-convicts is a good example of this collaboration (Moore 1978). However, more needs to be done, especially in the area of fieldwork, because students as well as faculty need valid data about the people they study, and they need to gather it in ways that are not offensive to the people.

Most of the research done on racial and ethnic groups in the United States has not been sensitive to the needs of the ethnic community, nor have systematic techniques been developed to make data collection more ethically responsible. Ethnic groups have been exploited by researchers in the past, and this contributes to the distrust that already exists between the dominant group and the subordinate minority groups. For example, a number of community members, that is, Samoans, mentioned that they would not like any research done on them that made them appear negative to the public or, in the case of African Americans, reinforced old myths and stereotypes about them. Some of these people were familiar with research that had been done on them in the past and they were very pessimistic about further research benefiting them. Community members usually do not have the means to discredit the researcher when he/she produces information on them that is not accurate in their eyes, so this raises the issue of research ethics and the commitment of the researcher. Should he fail to publish findings that are negative even though he considers them valid? This is a difficult question to answer, but it needs to be addressed when research is done. Of course, if there is a collaborative effort between community members and researchers, this problem would be less likely to occur because there would be active criticism and evaluation of the research from both an academic and community point of view.

Collaborative research can be done using a community-based participatory model where those who are being studied are actually asked about their opinions at all stages of research development The researcher includes different segments of a community in the research effort, he has them define the problems and issues, and he also has them come up with possible solutions that can be implemented. The researcher takes more of a backseat approach and allows the individuals in the community to instruct the researcher. This collaboration makes research a community effort.

Randy Stoecker's project-based research fits this model because it focuses on creating social change in a community that results in a real difference in people's lives. The model begins with diagnosing a problem or issue, developing a plan for intervening in the problem, putting the plan into action, and evaluating the results of the research to see if the desired change has occurred (2005, 8). Community-based research is also done between colleges and community groups, and it includes the following: a collaborative enterprise between academic researchers (professors and students) and community members, a validation of multiple sources of knowledge together with the promotion of multiple methods of discovery and the dissemination of knowledge from the research, and the goal of social action and social change for the purpose of achieving social justice (Strand et al. 2003).

This approach would be the most inclusive in allowing community members to fully participate in research. It may not be appropriate for all types of research in ethnic communities, but it is the most accommodating. Another way to get wider community feedback into research concerns is to conduct focus groups (in-depth discussion sessions on a specific topic) at various stages of research. This is more time-consuming because it requires identifying likely participants, conducting the groups, and analyzing the results; but it can be beneficial in keeping the researcher in tune with community needs. Both of these approaches are most likely to be successful with ethnic groups that have been in the United States for a while. Recent immigrants may not have formed a sense of community awareness yet, and traditional ethnic groups may require a research approach that acknowledges the status hierarchy in the community.

The good news is that social scientists have been concerned about ethnic group research methodology since the 1970s, and Montero (1977) has been able to summarize some of the insights acquired from different studies that were done. These ideas include:

1. Getting acceptance from the community through a "snowball" effect where contact with one informant leads to another and then another. This can also happen by getting the sponsorship of a local or national ethnic association.
2. Formulating theoretical propositions about minority groups by getting "clues" from the field setting or from field notes.
3. Using fieldwork to sensitize the researcher to the parameters and nature of the ethnic community. This includes getting at the language, customs, and habits of the people so that any type of research, such as large scale surveys, are more in tune with the community.
4. Being sensitive to the problems of reliability and validity of the interview method, which can be compounded in the study of minority populations. This is especially critical where information is kept secret from the researcher.

5. Being aware of ethical concerns that may face the researcher about his or her role as an investigator. Especially critical are decisions about research findings that may stigmatize informants or the ethnic community.

Ethnic research, in order to be successful, must take into consideration the feelings, thoughts, perceptions, and customs of the people. This has not been done in the majority of cases where sociological studies have been done, perhaps because researchers have been from the dominant group and they saw ethnic members as subjects or objects of research rather than as collaborators. This has reinforced the in-group/out-group phenomenon between the majority group and minority groups that is so pervasive in American society. Not only has this division given us the illusion of accurate research results, but it has fostered greater distrust between groups. This book has attempted to correct this problem by addressing the issue of trust-distrust as a primary concern in research with ethnic communities. Distrust, though pervasive in our society, can lead to trust when interethnic relations are given as much attention as the actual research being done in communities. Though this may seem like more work for the researcher, the benefits should outweigh the costs as ethnic members begin to trust the outsider much more than before and show genuine interest in research projects.

# References

Abu-Lughod, Janet. 1961. "Migrant Adjustment to City Life (Egypt)." *American Journal of Sociology* 67:22–32.

Aguilera, M., and M. Emerson. 2005. "Inter-Racial and Intra-Racial Trust: the Determinants of Trust." Presented at the annual meeting of the Pacific Sociological Association, Portland, Oregon.

Anderson, Nels. 1923. *The Hobo: The Sociology of the Homeless Man.* Chicago: University of Chicago Press.

Bean, Roy A., Benjamin J. Perry, and Tina M. Bedell. 2001. "Developing Culturally Competent Marriage and Family Therapists: Guidelines for Working with Hispanic Families." *Journal of Marital and Family Therapy* 27(1):43–54.

Bonder, Bette, Laura Martin, and Andrew Miracle. 2001. "Achieving Cultural Competence: the Challenge for Clients and Healthcare Workers in a Multicultural Society." *Generations,* Spring:35–42.

Bunte, Pamela A., and Rebecca M. Joseph. 1992. "The Cambodian Community of Long Beach: An Ethnographic Analysis of Factors Leading to Census Undercount." *Ethnographic Evaluation of the 1990 Decennial Census Report Series, Report #9.* Washington D.C.: Center for Survey Methods Research, Bureau of the Census.

Chikahisa, Paul, Kay Cho, Arlene Hori Kushida, and Royal F. Morales. 1976. "Asian and Pacific American Curriculum on Social work Education." Asian American Community Mental Health Training Center. Los Angeles. Unpublished Manuscript.

Clark, Margaret. 1970. *Health in the Mexican-American Culture.* Berkeley: University of California Press.

Crawford, Ann C. 1980. "Vietnamese Customs and Rites." *SEAR: Multi–Lingual Dispatch* 2:12–14.

Cressey, Paul G. 1932. *The Taxi-Dance Hall: A Sociological Study in Commercialized Recreation and City Life.* Chicago: University of Chicago Press.

Durkheim, Emile. 1933. *The Division of Labor in Society.* New York: The Free Press.

171

Eames, E., and W. Schwab. 1964. "Urban Migration in India and Africa." *Human Organization* 23:24–7.

Erikson, Erik H. 1950. *Childhood and Society.* New York: W. W. Norton & Company, Inc.

Estrada, Leobardo F., F. Chris Garcia, Reynaldo Flores Macias, and Lionel Maldonado. "Chicanos in the United States: a History of Exploitation and Resistance." Pp. 177–187 in *Sources: Notable Selections in Race and Ethnicity,* edited by Adalberto Aguirre, Jr. and David Baker. Guilford, Conn.: the Dushkin Publishing Group, Inc.

Falicov, Celia J. 1996. "Mexican Americans." Pp. 229–41 in *Ethnicity and Family Therapy,* edited by M. McGoldrick, J. Giordano, and N. Garcia-Preto. New York: The Guilford Press.

Festinger, Leon, Henry W. Riecken, and Stanley Schachter. 1956. *When Prophecy Fails.* St. Paul, Minn.: University of Minnesota Press.

*Field Work Manual.* 1979. School of Social Work, University of Southern California, Los Angeles. Unpublished manuscript.

Filoiali'i, La'auli Ale. 1980. "Attitudes Toward the Traditional Fa'a Samoa As a Problem of Adjusting to Urban Life in America." Department of Public Administration, Pepperdine University, Los Angeles. Unpublished manuscript.

Glenn, Evelyn N., and Stacey G. H. Yap. 2002. "Chinese American Families." Pp. 134–163 in *Minority Families in the United States: A Multicultural Perspective,* edited by Ronald L. Taylor. Upper Saddle River, N.J.: Pearson Education, Inc.

Gomez, Rudolf. 1972. *The Changing Mexican-American.* El Paso, TX: University of Texas.

Gonzales Jr., Juan L. 1993. *Racial and Ethnic Groups in America.* Dubuque, Ia.: Kendall/Hunt Publishing Company.

Hammersley, Martyn, and Paul Atkinson. 1995. *Ethnography: Principles in Practice.* New York: Routledge.

Hang, Jim Quang. 1979. "The 'Boat People' The Vietnamese-Chinese." *SEAR: Multi-Lingual Dispatch* 1:18–20.

Harlow, Roxanna, and Lauren Dundes. 2004. "'United' We Stand: Responses to the September 11 Attacks in Black and White." *Sociological Perspectives* 47:439–464.

Henderson, Neil. 2005. "Models of Service Delivery for Minority Populations and Caregivers." Presented at the annual meeting of the Association for Gerontology in Higher Education, Oklahoma City.

Homans, George C. 1958. "Social Behavior As Exchange." *American Journal of Sociology* 63:597–606.

Ishizuka, K. C. 1978. *The Elder Japanese.* San Diego: Campanile Press.

Johnson, Jerry C., and Nancy H. Smith. 2002. "Health and Social Issues Associated With Racial, Ethnic, and Cultural Disparities." *Generations* Fall:25–32.

Junker, Buford, H. 1960. *Field Work: An Introduction to the Social Sciences.* Chicago: University of Chicago Press.

Kibria, Nazli. 2002. "Vietnamese Americans." Pp. 181–192 in *Minority Families in the United States: A Multicultural Perspective,* edited by Ronald L. Taylor. Upper Saddle River, N.J.: Pearson Education, Inc.

Kikumura, Akemi, and Harry H. L. Kitano. 1973. "Interracial Marriage: A Picture of the Japanese Americans." *The Journal of Social Issues* 29:67–81.

Kim, Elena Young–Kyong, Roy A. Bean, and James M. Harper. 2004. "Do General Treatment Guidelines for Asian American Families Have Applications to Specific Ethnic Groups? The Case of Culturally Competent Therapy With Korean Americans." *Journal of Marital and Family Therapy* 30:359–372.

Kitano, Harry. 1969. *Japanese Americans*. Englewood Cliffs, N.J.: Prentice-Hall, Inc.

Kluckhohn, Clyde, and Dorothea Leighton. 1962. *The Navajo*. Garden City, N.Y.: Doubleday & Company, Inc.

Kornblum, William. 1989. "On Studying South Chicago." Pp. 101–112 in *In the Field: Readings on the Field Experience,* edited by Carolyn D. Smith, and William Kornblum. New York: Praeger.

Kuykendall, Kenneth L. 1979. "Traditional Samoan Views on Death and Dying." Presented at the annual meeting of the Southwestern Anthropological Association, March, Santa Barbara, CA.

LaPiere, Richard T. 1934. "Attitudes vs. Actions." *Social Forces* XIII:230–37.

Leung, Paul K., and James Boehnlein. 1996. "Vietnamese Families." Pp. 295–306 in *Ethnicity and Family Therapy,* edited by Monica McGoldrick, Joe Giordano, and John K.Pearce. New York: The Guilford Press.

Liebow, Elliot. 1967. *Tally's Corner: A Study of Negro Streetcorner Men*. Boston: Little, Brown & Co.

———. 1989. "A Field Experience in Retrospect." Pp. 35–44 in *In the Field: Readings On the Field Research Experience,* edited by Carolyn D. Smith, and William Kornblum. New York: Praeger.

Lyman, Stanford. 1970. *Asian in the West*. Social Science and Humanities Publication Number 4, Las Vegas, Nev.: University of Nevada System.

Mai, Dr. Tran Van. 1975. "Cross-Cultural Understanding and its Implications in Counseling." Indochina Social Services Project, Los Angeles. Unpublished manuscript.

Martinez, Ricardo Arguijo. 1978. *Hispanic Culture and Health Care*. St Louis: The C. V. Mosby Company.

Matejko, Alexander J., and Steven D. Williams. 1993. "Building Trust in Interethnic Encounters." *Canadian Ethnic Studies* 25(2):1–14.

Mead, Margaret. 1928. *Coming of Age in Samoa*. New York: Morrow.

McLemore, S. Dale. 1991. *Racial and Ethnic Relations in America*. Needham Heights, Mass.: Allyn & Bacon.

Min, Pyong Gap. 2002. "Korean American Families." Pp. 193–211 in *Minority Families in the United States: A Multicultural Perspective,* edited by Ronald L. Taylor. Upper Saddle River, N.J.: Pearson Education, Inc.

Mindel, Charles H., Robert W. Habenstein, and Roosevelt Wright, Jr. 1998. *Ethnic Families in America: Patterns and Variations*. Upper Saddle River, N.J.: Prentice Hall.

Miner, Horace. 1956. "Body Ritual among the Nacirema." *American Anthropologist* 58:503–507.

Miyamoto, Frank. 1939. "Social Solidarity among the Japanese in Seattle." *University of Washington Publications in the Social Sciences* II(2):57–130.

———. 1973. "The Forced Evacuation of the Japanese Minority During World War II." *The Journal of Social Issues* 29:11–31.

Montero, Darrel. 1977. "Research among Racial and Cultural Minorities: An Overview." *Journal of Social Issues* 33:1–10.

———. 1979. "The Vietnamese Refugees in America: Toward a Theory of Spontaneous International Migration." *International Migration Review* 13(4):624–648.

———. 1981. "Vietnamese Assimilation in American Society." Pp. 119–139 in *New Directions in Ethnic Studies: Minorities in America, edited by David Claerbaut. Saratoga, CA: Century Twenty One Publishing.*

Moore, Joan. 1978. *Homeboys.* Philadelphia: Temple University Press.

Moore, Joan W. 1969. *Mexican Americans.* Englewood Cliffs, N.J.: Prentice-Hall, Inc.

Muir, J., Schwartz, S., and Szapocznik, J. 2004. "A Program of Research with Hispanic and African American Families: Three decades of Intervention Development and Testing Influenced by the Changing Cultural Context of Miami." *Journal of Marital and Family Therapy* 30(3):285–303.

Murdock, G. P. et al. 1971. *Outline of Cultural Materials.* Behavioral Science Outlines, Vol. I., New Haven, Conn.: Human Relations Area Files, Inc.

Murry, Velma McBride, and Gene H. Brody. 2004. "Partnering with Community Stakeholders: Engaging Rural African American Families in Basic Research and the Strong African American Families Preventive Intervention Program." *Journal of Marital and Family Therapy* 30(3): 271–283.

Nghiem, Tong. 1979. "Something About Vietnamese Cultural Aspect." *SEAR: Multi-Lingual Dispatch* I(8/9/10):14–15.

Okano, Yukio. 1976. "Japanese Americans and Mental Health: An Exploratory Study of Attitudes." Ph.D. dissertation, California School of Professional Psychology, Los Angeles.

Pelto Pertti. 1978. *Anthropological Research: The Structure of Inquiry.* Cambridge: Cambridge University Press.

Perez, Michael P. 2005. "Colonialism, Americanization, and Indigenous Identity: A Research Note on Chomorro Identity in Guam." *Sociological Spectrum* 25:571–591.

Pinkney, Alphonso. 1969. *Black Americans.* Englewood Cliffs, N.J.: Prentice-Hall, Inc.

Redfield, Robert. 1947. "The Folk Society." *American Journal of Sociology* 52:293–308.

Ritter, Marion, and Theresa Ward Warner. 1980. "Cultural Traditions II: The People of Laos." *Indochinese Refugee Reports* May 20:1–4.

Schatzman, Leonard, and Anselm L. Strauss. 1973. *Field Research: Strategies for a Natural Sociology.* Englewood Cliffs, N.J.: Prentice-Hall, Inc.

Shelley, N. Mark. 2001. "Building Community from 'Scratch': Forces at Work among Urban Vietnamese Refugees in Milwaukee." *Sociological Inquiry* 71:473–92.

Shu, Ramsay, and Adele Salamasina Satele. 1977. "The Samoan Community in Southern California: Conditions and Needs." Asian American Mental Health Research Center, Chicago. Unpublished manuscript.

Stoecker, Randy. 2005. *Research Methods for Community Change: A Project-Based Approach.* Thousand Oaks, CA: Sage Publications.

Strand, Kerry, Sam Marullo, Nick Culforth, Randy Stoecker, and Patrick Donohue. 2003. *Community-Based Research and Higher Education.* San Francisco: Jossey-Bass.

Sunstein, Bonnie Stone, and Elizabeth Chiseri-Strater. 2002. *Fieldworking: Reading and Writing Research.* Boston: Bedford/St. Martin's.

Takagi, Dana Y. 2002. "Japanese American Families." Pp. 164–180 in *Minority Families in the United States: A Multicultural Perspective,* edited by Ronald L. Taylor. Upper Saddle River, N.J.: Pearson Education, Inc.

Thinh, Dinh Van. 1979. "The Indochinese Refugees: An Introduction to Their Culture." Department of Social Services pamphlet, State of Utah.

Tonnies, Ferdinand. 1957. *Community and Society.* Translated by Charles P. Loomis. East Lansing: Michigan State University Press.

Turner, William L., Elizabeth Wieling, and William D. Allen. 2004. "Developing Culturally Effective Family-Based Research Programs: Implications for Family Therapists." *Journal of Marital & Family Therapy* 30(3):257–270.

Ui, Shiori. 1991. "Unlikely Heroes: the Evolution of Female Leadership in a Cambodian Ethnic Enclave." Pp. 161–177 in *Ethnography Unbound: Power and Resistance in the Modern Metropolis,* edited by Burawoy, Michael et al. Berkeley: University of California Press.

Waddell, J. O., and O. M. Watson. 1971. *The American Indian in Urban Society.* New York: Little, Brown & Co.

Wax, Rosalie. 1971. *Doing Fieldwork: Warnings and Advice.* Chicago: University of Chicago Press.

Weaver, Hilary N. 2005. *Explorations in Cultural Competence: Journeys to the Four Directions.* Belmont, CA: Thomson Brooks/Cole.

Welch, Michael R., Roberta E. N. Rivera, Brian P. Conway, Jennifer Yonkoski, Paul M. Lupton, and Russell Giancola. 2005. "Determinants and Consequences of Social Trust." *Sociological Inquiry* 75:453–473.

White, M., and Epston, D. 1990. *Narrative Means to Therapeutic Ends.* New York: Norton.

Williams, Thomas Rhys. 1967. *Field Methods in the Study of Culture.* New York: Holt, Rinehart and Winston.

# Appendix

## Interview Schedule and Questionnaire
## Pilot Ethnic Research Training
## Project (1980)

Directions: for each person interviewed, please obtain the following information.

1. Name:
2. Sex:
3. Age:
4. Number of years in the United States
5. Occupation

Interview Questions for Ethnic Community Members[1]

1. How does your community regard the university (i.e., with respect or with irritation)
2. How does your community regard university people (students and/or professors) doing research in your community?
3. What areas of research would be legitimate for your community? Valuable?
4. How much research would be acceptable to do in your community? Is there a point at which research becomes a nuisance to members of your community?
5. In what ways would you want to be informed about the research and/or participate?
6. What is the worst thing a student or professor could do in your community?

---

[1]These interview questions were spread out in questionnaire format so that the respondent could write in his/her answers in narrative form rather than having the interviewer do all the writing.

7. How should the researcher behave around different types of members of your ethnic community (i.e., the young, the elderly, the lower class, upper class, men/women, husbands/wives, etc.)?
8. What is the proper courtesy that a stranger from outside your community should display when first meeting members of your community?
9. What are some of the common cultural beliefs and traditions that the researcher should know about before going into your community?

# Index

Breinigsville, PA USA
07 December 2010
250780BV00001B/2/P